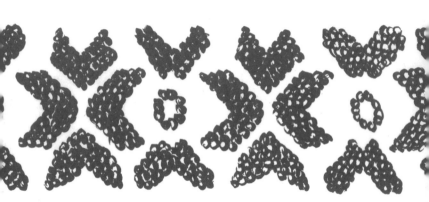

HOW TO BE DANISH

HOW TO BE DANISH

FROM LEGO TO LUND: A SHORT INTRODUCTION
TO THE STATE OF DENMARK

PATRICK KINGSLEY

Illustrations by Karoline Kirchhübel Andersen

This book was first published in 2012 by
Short Books
3A Exmouth House
Pine Street
EC1R 0JH

10 9 8 7 6 5 4 3 2

A CIP catalogue record for this book
is available from the British Library.

ISBN 978-1-78072-133-0

Printed and bound by CPI Group (UK) Ltd, Croydon, CR0 4YY

CONTENTS

CONTENTS

DENMARK

INTRODUCTION

There was a point early in 2012 when it felt as if you couldn't open a British newspaper or magazine without reading something about Denmark. We read that the Danes are the happiest people in the world – the UN said so. There were paeans to BBC4's cult Danish dramas – not just *The Killing*, but *Borgen* and *The Bridge*, which was watched by over a million people in Britain. There were interviews with Helle Thorning-Schmidt, Denmark's first female prime minister, and reams of writing about Noma, named the world's best restaurant for the third year in a row. For the first half of 2012, the Danes were the presidents of the EU, which gave them even greater exposure. We heard eulogies to their utopian welfare state, their unrivalled cycling culture and their commitment to environmentalism. Some of us remembered Denmark for the Muhammed cartoons crisis of 2006. The rest of us donned as many layers as we could of Danish knitwear. In short, Scandi fever – or perhaps more accurately,

Danish delirium – gripped the nation. Or parts of it, anyway.

In one sense, *How to be Danish* is yet another drop in the deluge. In another, it's an attempt to connect the dots between some of the different puddles. Part reportage, part travelogue, it can't be the definitive book about Danish life. But using shows like *The Killing* as a starting point, it will hopefully provide a wider context to the bits of Denmark that over the past few years have intrigued some of us in Britain – an accessible panorama of contemporary Danish life, written from an English perspective. In spring 2012, I spent a month in Denmark, travelling from the cycling lanes of Copenhagen to the windmills of west Jutland. I visited the set of *The Killing*, the test labs of the New Nordic kitchen and the place that's said to be the happiest town in the world. I poked around mosques and schools, churches and farms – and a remote little island where some grizzled farmers have created the world's most unlikely eco-haven. I interviewed over 70 Danes – most of them fascinating, a few of them dull; many of them in the public eye, but some not. I bounced from actors to designers, chefs to architects, journalists, politicians, students, imams, refugees – feeling my way as I went. I met the people who created Sarah Lund, the man who founded Noma, and the woman who knitted *that* jumper. This book is a stab at creating a narrative from some of those encounters. It is not – in case anyone has read too much into the title – a serious tutorial on how, actually, to be Danish. Most countries are impenetrable to outsiders, but some – like, perhaps, America – have a national identity that is at least semi-permeable to newcomers. Denmark is not yet one of them.

Four per cent of Danes are called Larsen. According to some estimates, just 3% are Muslim: it is still a fairly homogenous country. For reasons that will hopefully become clear in later chapters, Danishness is still something that can only really be achieved through a Danish upbringing – and definitely not from a short book like this. It's a small place, Denmark. Many Danish micro-worlds bleed into others, and as a result it is hard to construct a thread about the country within clearly compartmentalised chapters. I've written eight. While each one is rooted in a single theme – respectively: education, food, design, politics, identity, Copenhagen, television, Jutland – they all often meander into other realms. The politics chapter begins with a discussion about the Danish language, but stick with it. The section on Copenhagen is also the story of Danish bicycles and architecture. Knitting creeps into the strand about television. The last chapter kicks off in Jutland, with some teenagers pissing against a wall, but ends up talking about windmills. All of them, though, can be read on their own. *God fornøjelse*!

1. WORK WELL, PLAY WELL:
a Scandinavian education

"Everyone has to take part" – Else Mathiassen

It could be any old school disco. In the sports hall, the cool kids bounce around to loud music. In the playground, the shy ones look at their shoes, shivering. At some point, a young woman wrapped in an inflatable orange tube bursts from the sports hall and pinballs across the playground, aiming a large yellow water gun at all those who cross her path. This is the end-of-year party at Ingrid Jespersen High School – theme: "beach"; weather: Danish – but not all of those present share their classmate's exuberance. It's a cold night, and perhaps they regret obeying the Hawaiian dress code with quite such diligence.

Some feet away in the sports hall, a few hundred other sixth-formers are having a better time of it. Ringed with garlands of fake flowers, they bump to Rihanna, and Danish artists like Kidd and Malk de Koijn. Every so often they'll thrust their way towards the makeshift bar where their teachers – known, like all Danish teachers, by their first names – happily hand out pints of beer. In the corners, couples make out. People are merry, but not blotto. In a last hurrah before next week's exams, most of them are having fun. Still, something makes me anxious. First up, I feel like I've been here before. Second: I keep thinking that something unspeakably evil is about to happen.

In a way, I'm partly right. I have been here before – at least, I've seen this place on screen. It's the playground where they filmed the school scenes from the first season of *The Killing*. Much of the plot of the first few episodes revolves around what happens one night at a school disco – a disco, slightly disconcertingly, that is rather like this one. At first, you think a girl's been kidnapped at the party. Then you think she's been murdered in the basement. Finally, you suspect someone else has been raped – or, at the very least, filmed having group sex. I look around. Where's the camera? Where's the basement? Who's the killer? But these aren't the only questions I'm wrestling with. I came here tonight fascinated mostly by the school's connections to Danish television. I've ended up just as intrigued by what the school says about the Danish education system, and, in fact, Denmark itself.

In a way, Ingrid Jespersen is not very representative of Denmark at all. It's quite elitist, in fact. It's a private school, it's in a posh bit of Copenhagen and the offspring of three very different, very high-profile politicians all go here – the daughter of the social democratic prime minister; the daughter of the leader of the Danish Lib Dems; and the grandchild of Pia Kjaersgaard, the one-time leader of – for want of a better comparison – the Danish equivalent of the BNP.

But as Rihanna throbs away in the background, one thing fascinates me. If this is a private school, why does the government subsidise around 80% of the school fees?

•

It's sometimes claimed that Denmark is a classless society. While this is obviously a sizeable exaggeration – as the fictional prime minister in *Borgen* says, "It's a myth that we're all equal" – a lot of the state apparatus is nevertheless tilted towards lessening social divisions. The subsidy for private education is a good example of this. It's given to all those who want to study privately in Denmark, and accordingly it shows you both how large the Danish state is – and how committed that state is to creating equality. True, the students at Ingrid Jespersen come, on the whole, from wealthier backgrounds than their counterparts at Danish state schools. But they also represent a far wider social range than those at an equivalent private school in Britain. Twelve hours before the disco got going, I spent the morning interviewing a class that was at the end of their second year of three at Ingrid Jespersen. Put your hands up, I said, if you would struggle to come here without the subsidy. Around half the class did – which tells its own story. "If my parents had to pay for everything at this school, I couldn't afford to come," says one, an 18-year-old called Rasmus. Like many youngsters in Denmark, he speaks very precise, almost flawless English. "We don't have that money. The state covers most of the expenses." Naturally, places like this are still seen as elitist – but they don't have quite the same stigma that they do in Britain, and they're much more mixed.

The knock-on effect is that as a group the students are more grounded and more socially conscious than you'd expect their British equivalents to be. A while back, Class 2B went on an exchange to a private school in Scotland, which shall remain nameless. Put simply, they were shocked at the social divisions they came across there. "In Scotland, they mentioned 'working class'," remembers Rasmus, sitting next to a shelf of test tubes. "In Denmark, of course we have that, but the difference is not very great. You can go from working class to upper class if you get a good job. And if you get an education you should be able to get a good job." It also helps that the wage disparity between different jobs is not particularly large, which means that Danes are less snooty about what jobs people do. "I don't look down upon any specific jobs," says Rasmus. "If you left school at 16 and became a garbage man, it might pay almost as good as a doctor. It's not easy, but you can do it." Again, this is an exaggeration – but the broad gist is correct. Thanks to the strength of the Danish trade unions, a doctor earns on average only twice as much as a refuse collector, a judge only two and a half times more than a cleaner. According to the Gini index, which measures income disparity, the gap between rich and poor in Denmark is currently the lowest in the world.

It's important not to read too much into what one class of Danes thought of one class of Scots (and it would be amusing to hear what the Scots thought of the Danes) but their thoughts are useful in that they hint at what's different about Danish education, and, by extension, Danish society.

"When you compare us to other EU countries, our education is very badly rated," says 17-year-old Augusta. "We're not brought up to learn things by heart. But if you ask Danish students and Danish children about politics, we're more reflective. We have more of our own views. We think more about our society. We sensed in Scotland that they are taught in a more old-fashioned way."

You could argue that this approach starts from the age of six months. At this point in a Danish child's life, state-subsidised childcare kicks in – which means that parents pay no more than 25% of the cost of sending their child to nursery (around £300 a month). If they're low earners, they pay far less – and in turn this means that everyone can and does put their children in childcare from an early age. This has two main effects. It encourages the vast majority of women to go back to work. Over 70% of Danish mothers are in work – in Britain, that figure falls to 55%. Second, it means that children from the age of six months are a) separated from their parents for large parts of the day; and b) surrounded by kids of all backgrounds.

There are many criticisms of these nurseries; one common view is that the education they provide is not structured enough. But their many supporters argue that they teach Danish children to be more independent, and, by introducing them to other people from all walks of life, they also make them aware of the importance of society, and of cooperating with your equals – a recurrent theme in Denmark, and, in fact, this book. Only in Denmark could there be a board game – Konsensus – based around the concept of collaboration. It's no coincidence that the name of the Danes' most famous export – Lego toys – is derived from the Danish words "leg godt". Play well.

This focus on independence extends outside the school gates, too. Since cycling and cycling infrastructure are so widespread, children are often allowed to roam around town at a younger age than they might do abroad. "Our parents don't have to drive us," says Søren, a chap with the beginnings of some lengthy dreadlocks. "We take care of our

own transportation from an early age. We don't have to have a driving licence to get around. At ten or 11, you can go to a lot of places yourself on your bike. It's normal to do it at nine." A quarter of children aged between seven and 14 have part-time jobs.

Teenagers can also get their hands on alcohol much more easily – and in fact they drink more alcohol per capita than youngsters in any other country. You can buy booze as early as 16, and people aren't prompted for their ID as often as they are in other countries. Meanwhile parents often give their 14-year-olds cans of beer to take to a party – an attempt to moderate their drinking without banning it completely. Opinion is divided as to the effect this all has. Predictably some think it encourages binging; others argue the opposite – that it makes alcohol less of an issue. "I think we drink differently to how they do in the UK," argues Benedicte, 17. "The people going out there – they were drunk. They were REALLY drunk. We tend to just get tipsy." Some of her classmates argue that the class's attitude to binging is unusual. But most of them claim it's standard for Danes their age – that while Danish teens drink more often, they usually do it in moderation, and in less pressurised circumstances.

In a year or two, this class will start to think about university. The decision they face is different from that faced by students in Britain. Here, there has been a fierce debate about whether the rise in university fees from £9000 to £27,000 will prove off-putting to those from poorer backgrounds. In Denmark, that premise seems farcical. University education is entirely free. In fact, Danish students are in a sense paid to go to university: they receive around £500 a month in living expenses. It's a different mentality. Students aren't seen as a burden on the state, but as people whose skills will one day support it. They're future participants in Danish life, and they're treated as such. Every effort is made to make them better able to participate.

In Denmark, a well-rounded personality is seen as a key component of this ability to participate, which helps explain the existence of two very Danish institutions that have few overseas equivalents: the continuation school, and the folk high school. The former is the state-subsidised boarding school where many 16-year-olds go to study in the year before they leave for sixth form. They follow a basic academic curriculum, but the main focus is on creativity. Some continuation schools specialise in sport, others centre on drama and art, and some are essentially music schools. Their sole goals are to develop the students' extra-curricular interests, and to help them – at a pivotal moment in their lives – mature as human beings. The folk high school is a very similar concept, but it's aimed at those who have already left school – adults of any age, in fact – and there are no exams.

"It's part of this Danish tradition that everyone has to take part in political life, or in life in general," says Else Mathiassen, who runs the West Jutland folk high school. "Each individual should be developed in his or her own way – but also know how to function within a group. And to do that, you need to be enlightened! You have to be personally enlightened in order to know about society today. To enable you to be part of the democracy that we have."

It's easy to be cynical about such idealism. As the

fictional leader of the Social Democrats admits in *Borgen*: "People don't run anything." But walking around the grounds of the high school, you can see why Else's so inspired. We're halfway up the coast of the North Sea — as far from Copenhagen as you can really get in Denmark — and the place is dreamy. At its centre is an airy hub of bedrooms and workshops that open out onto acres of gardens and woodland. A blue tit flutters about the art studio, and the vegetable patches are stuffed with potatoes and lemon balm. In the woods in the distance, sculptures made by recent students poke from the trees. The whole estate smells of spring.

There are 70 of these places in Denmark, and one in ten Danish adults — with half of their fees paid for by the state — will spend a spell at one at some point in their lives. Most people tend to come in their twenties, but parents and pensioners often enrol too. In fact, the schools hold such a special place in the Danish identity that Else thinks that the very elderly sometimes come here to pass away. "Sometimes older people die here, and I have to ring up the family to break them the news," she explains. "Often they'll say: 'Oh, that's nice, he obviously wanted to die in a folk high school.'" Each school has its own specialism — West Jutland is particularly known for its focus on eco-living — but all of them will teach dancing, writing, ceramics, painting, acting, cooking, gardening, debating and philosophy. The last two are particularly important because the ability to articulate an argument is a key part of being an active citizen.

This highly democratic approach to education is not a recent Danish phenomenon. It can be seen in the context of a wider drive towards social democracy that began in Denmark around 150 years ago. The roots of Danish educational ideology, like many Danish concepts, can be traced to the mid-1800s, when the country was in the process of losing much of its southern (and historically German) territory to a newly belligerent Prussia. In 1864, Denmark finally surrendered its two southernmost provinces, Schleswig and Holstein, to Prussia, a defeat which saw the country lose 40% of its population. It was a moment of huge national trauma. Until that point, Denmark still rather optimistically saw itself as a relatively powerful, multinational commonwealth,

Nikolai Grundtvig

despite having regularly lost large parts of its empire since the 1500s. But in 1864, with the loss of their last significant annex, the Danes had finally to accept that their once-vast medieval empire – a Baltic sprawl that had housed several states and a babble of languages – was in fact now just one single, tiny monoculture. This prompted a national identity crisis, and forced Danes to reassess the values that united them.

The debate was heavily influenced by the ideas of a man called Nikolai Grundtvig, who is now considered a Danish national hero. By the late 1840s, Denmark had finally made the transition from absolute monarchy to parliamentary monarchy. In very simplistic terms, Grundtvig – a priest, thinker, and sometime politician active from the 1830s onwards – felt that the new democratic system would work only if every Dane was able to participate in political life, and if, by extension, Danish society was made more egalitarian. From 1838, as the campaign for democracy gathered pace, he gave a series of lectures promoting the concept of what he coined *folkelighed*, or what the historian Knud Jespersen translates as a "mutually committed community". Grundtvig, writes Jespersen in his highly recommended *A History of Denmark*, "was particularly concerned with the question of how to transform the hitherto inarticulate general public into responsible citizens in the coming democracy – in other words, to turn the humble subjects of the king into good democrats".

His arguments had a huge effect. "In virtually every area

imaginable," says Jespersen, "the ideas developed by Grundtvig and his circle at a particular historical point in the middle of the nineteenth century have left a deep and long-lasting impression on the Danish psyche and on the way in which Danish society operates today. This is not necessarily because any of these ideas were in themselves especially original, but because at a critical crossroads in the history of Denmark, he was able to formulate his thoughts in such ways as to create a great impact and a comprehensive pro-gramme of action able to change the humble subjects or an absolute monarch into more mature members of a demo-cratic society and at the same time unite the inhabitants of the remains of the Oldenborg state [the once mighty Danish empire] as one people, a Danish nation. The key concepts in this were *folkelighed*, tolerance, openness and liberal-mind-edness: the means were enlightenment and committed dia-logue."

Indeed, Grundtvig was (and is) so revered in Denmark that when he died, a whole new suburb of Copenhagen, with a gargantuan church at its centre, was designed in his honour. The church (built, as it happens, by the father of Kaare Klint, whom we will meet in two chapters' time, and filled with chairs by Klint himself) is quite a shock at first sight. You reach it by winding through several quiet resi-dential terraces before – bam! – you're hit by this vast juke-box of a building, a triangular man-made cliff-face that is three or four times the height of its po-faced neighbours.

Grundtvig's first practical aim was to give all Danes

access to a thorough, humanist education, particularly in isolated areas traditionally ignored by the Copenhagen elite. Thus Grundtvig set about founding what became known as folk high schools – liberal arts colleges for the rural poor that now survive in the more arts-focussed form described above.

"The goal," writes Jespersen, "was to offer young people the chance to stay in a school during the winter, where inspirational teachers and the living word could awaken their dormant spirit and sharpen their perceptions. In short the intent was no less than to transform the inarticulate masses into responsible and articulate citizens in the new democratic society which was slowly taking shape."

The first folk high school was built in 1844 in a village in south Jutland. By 1864, there were 14 – and in 1874 there were 50. Now there are 70.

As Denmark sought to redefine itself in the years following 1864, concepts like the folk high schools and *folkelighed* began to take root in the Danish psyche. Danish farmers and dairymen – many of whom went to a folk high school and had consequently been imbued with a sense of both their own worth and their responsibility to society – clubbed together to form agrarian cooperatives that shared expensive materials, machinery and profits. For the first time in Danish history, these co-ops – inspired by a system pioneered by some weavers in Rochdale, Yorkshire – enabled the farmers to create meat and dairy products that were of a standard consistent enough to be exported. In time,

Denmark's farming community became not only one of the world's most prolific producers of bacon and butter (think: Lurpak), but also the foundation stone for the massive welfare state that gradually emerged in Denmark from the late 19th century onwards.

The folk high schools moved towards a more arts-based curriculum during the 60s, but their presence is testament to the enduring legacy of Grundtvig. Today, 75 students are enrolled at West Jutland – the school's biggest cohort ever. Else puts this down to the fact that the financial crisis has turned people from consumerism towards more wholesome activities. "People are starting to think in a more old-fashioned way," she explains. "They realise there are other ways of living, that it's not all about making money." But the crisis has also had a more negative effect. The government has cut some of its funding for the folk high schools, which means that students receive a slightly smaller subsidy. In turn, this makes it harder for poorer Danes to attend – it still costs around £120 a week – and so reduces the school's role as a social leveller.

Another problem is that folk high schools attract very few immigrants. The relationship between so-called

The Højskole (folk high school) logo

indigenous Danes and those whose families arrived only in the last three decades is often vexed. It reached its nadir during the Muhammed cartoons crisis of 2006, when a Danish newspaper published pictures that portrayed the Muslim prophet as a terrorist – sparking protests across the Arab world. How to foster integration is a constant source of debate in Denmark – and for her part, Else thinks it could be partly achieved if more so-called New Danes studied at schools like hers.

"Unfortunately, there are almost no immigrants here," she says. "It's a shame. It's a pity. I have been trying to get some to come. I think immigrants are brought up in this tradition that if you go to a school, you should end up with a paper so you can become a lawyer or a doctor. Here you end up with nothing! But I would love them to come here because they would know much more about Danish culture. If they came here, where you live together and eat together, they would so quickly learn how Danish people think."

But how *do* Danes think? They're a people deeply committed to cooperation and equality – and yet their third largest political party is from the far right. Their national hero preached tolerance – and yet it is the country that spawned the Muhammed cartoons. They're sometimes called the Latinos of Scandinavia – but drunk pedestrians will still wait patiently for a green man at four in the morning. Danes certainly aren't the warlike Viking progeny some Britons vaguely imagine them to be. But their values – and their character – are more complex than they first appear.

2. RAMSONS & SEAWEED:
the Nordic food revolution

"I felt that there was a relation between the lack of love or care, and the terrible food in Denmark. And in France I saw the opposite – an abundance of love and generosity, and taste and smell and great meals..." – Claus Meyer

Lars Williams stands at the stove and fries a chunk of mould. Every so often, the kitchen heaves to one side. We're on a houseboat in the Copenhagen harbour, and the occasional waves make cooking difficult. When winter comes, the days will be dark and short – but at least the kitchen won't roll in the frozen sea. After some minutes, Lars takes the fried mould from the frying pan and places it on a plate. From a box, he plucks a large, dead insect, and pops it on top – fried barley mould, served with grasshopper. "Breakfast," he says, and hands it to me.

It's no ordinary breakfast, but then this is no ordinary

kitchen. This is the Nordic Food Lab, an independent, non-profit laboratory where Lars and his team conduct obscure culinary experiments in the name of New Nordic cuisine – a much-chronicled movement founded in Denmark in 2004 to promote the use within Scandinavian cooking of local and seasonal produce. Eight years on, the lab is just one small part of a now fizzing Danish restaurant scene that is widely considered the most innovative in the world. The lab is an informal testing ground for restaurants like Relæ, Geist and Geranium in Copenhagen; Malling and Schmidt in Aarhus; and Ti Trin Ned in Fredericia – all founded since 2004, and now flagbearers for the New Nordic school. Many of them now have Michelin stars.

But first and foremost, there's Noma, a restaurant that stands barely 20 metres from the moorings of the Nordic Food Lab. Named the world's best restaurant for the past three years in a row, Noma is the flagship for the New Nordic movement, eschewing foreign goods like olive oil in favour of locally foraged flavours and herbs. Their aim is to recreate the geography and history of Scandinavia in food form. Ramsons, beach dandelions, sea buckthorn and sea lettuce – they're all plucked daily from the fields and shores surrounding Copenhagen by the chef Rene Redzepi and his team, or by an ever-larger troupe of professional foragers. Noma's meats and fish come from nearby farms and fisher-men, some of the wine from a little island called Lilleø in southern Denmark. Their sea urchins are snagged by a mad Scot who plunges into the Norwegian sea barely hours before his catch arrives on your plate. Redzepi himself serves some of the food, which is often characterised by a playful theatricality: eggs that the diner fries in a pan on her placemat; vegetables served in a trough of earth.

If you're not a foodie, the mania that surrounds the restaurant may surprise you. Saturdays at Noma often have a 1000-strong waiting list. You can only book a table on the first day of the month, and even then only for a date three months in the future. Needless to say, I couldn't get a table – but I spoke to people who have. "It's like experiencing a play in which you take an active part from the moment you step in the door," explains Bi Skaarup, president of the Danish Gastronomic Association. "Some of those three-star Michelin restaurants make you sit on the edge of your chair. You're afraid. But Noma is very relaxed. They peel the nervousness out of you. Rene is there himself. Although when we wanted to thank him at the end of the meal, he had already left because his wife was having a caesarean. He was there right up until the point he really needed to go to the hospital."

Bent Christensen has been writing guidebooks about Danish restaurants since the 70s, but his voice still quavers when he describes Noma. "Are you interested in football?" he asks when we meet. "Do you know how Barcelona play football? Do you see their passes? That's Noma. That's the service of Noma. Normally a restaurant's service is one of its weak points. Especially in the Nordic countries." His voice stretches to a higher pitch. "But at Noma they can DO it!" There is a pause while Bent fetches a wine delivery from the car park, but on his return he seems more emotional. "The food gives joy! It gives surprises. It gives a little bit of fear. You don't really know what to say when you see three little shrimps, still alive. But you are not there to be full in your stomach. You are not there to survive. You are there to have a very special experience."

In the press, Redzepi is treated like a god. A food blogger has called this the era of the "I Foraged with Rene Redzepi Piece", and the chef was recently seen on the cover of *Time*, having been named by the magazine as one of the world's most influential people. The adulation is not undeserved, but at the same time it obscures a much bigger story. For the narrative of the extraordinary culinary revival in Denmark goes far beyond just one man, or just one restaurant, or even the wider crop of restaurants mentioned earlier. Noma is just a part of how Denmark's entire food culture – from its bakeries to its farms, from its wholesalers to its consumers – has been transformed in the space of barely two decades from a bland backwater to the envy of the culinary world. Once they ate cheap foreign takeaways; now both consumers and wholesalers are increasingly interested in things grown and cooked on Danish soil.

You don't have to go to Noma to see it happening. You can visit Aamanns, in central Copenhagen, where a young chef has revitalised the dead Danish art of the open sandwich. You can pop into most supermarkets, where you'll find boxes and boxes of locally sourced ramsons, or wild garlic. This would have been unthinkable four or five years ago, when most people hadn't heard of the herb, and those who had might have thought it a weed. But with the rise of New Nordic cuisine, and with several restaurants now serving it, consumer demand for ramsons has quickly risen, and in many supermarkets you can buy 100 grams' worth for around 17 kroner. In some places, you can even buy stinging nettles. What's more, people aren't just buying these herbs; they're foraging for them too. One of Denmark's largest food organisations was recently so inundated with queries from the public about where to find both ramsons and seaweed that they have been forced to publish an online foraging guide to both. And sales have spiked for cookbooks like Claus Meyer's *Almanak*, which has a seasonal recipe for each day of the year and tells readers where to forage for weeds. The book has sold over 60,000 copies – the equivalent of selling 700,000 in Britain.

High-end bakeries – once almost extinct in Denmark – have re-emerged in the shape of chains like Emerys and Meyers, a response to the wave of homebaking that has swept the country in the last decade. Meanwhile, on a little island amusingly named Lolland, thousands are also flocking to an organic farm called Knuthenlund, whose recent transition mirrors that of Danish food culture in general. Once just like any other bland dairy farm, in 2007 Knuthenlund underwent the largest conversion to organic farming in Danish history, and now makes some of the most delicate cheeses in Europe. In 2011, 35,000 foodies made the slog to the remote farm to see what the fuss was about – 5000 more than would typically visit the Museum of Copenhagen each year in the noughties. The big dairies are getting in on the act too. Arla, who make much of the milk and butter we consume every day at breakfast, have long been criticised for their bland products and disregard for diversity and innovation. But the New Nordic movement has got Arla thinking.

"Ten years ago, some of the top chefs claimed that we didn't produce quality," admits John Gynther, the Arla executive who develops their new range of bespoke cheeses. "They said we only produced for the big consumers, discount chains and supermarkets. So ten years ago, we invited the chefs to meet us. We were of the opinion that our Lurpak butter was one of the most excellent butters in the world. 'Yes,' they said, 'but can you produce butter that reflects the change in seasons? That expresses the climate and landscapes here in the Nordic countries?' And they were right, we hadn't been working with innovation in this way. So we began to try it."

Initially, the project hit the buffers because Arla's massive factories simply weren't set up to make these kinds of bespoke products. But little by little, Gynther found ways of making smallscale production work. He trialled some niche Arla cheeses in some of the New Nordic restaurants – something that would previously have seemed unimaginable – and, ten years on, he is now on the verge of releasing, for high-end supermarkets, small ranges of bespoke cheeses

– some of them unpasteurised – that are distinctly Danish in their ingredients, and which come from specific farms or regions. "Do you know the New Nordic manifesto?" asks Gynther – an extraordinary question from a man whose company was once associated with the most uncreative aspects of Danish food. "That's my bible."

He's not just referring to the general ideas of the New Nordic kitchen. He means a very specific document that was drawn up in 2004 by Rene Redzepi and Claus Meyer, the author of *Almanak*, the owner of Meyers bakery and the man who founded Noma in the first place. Recognising that Scandinavia had long lacked a regional culinary identity, the pair decided they were going to create one.

"We weren't obsessed with being the best restaurant in the world at that point," remembers Meyer. "Rene and I at that moment wanted to make a great food culture in this region where the culinary legacy is so sad."

He was inspired not just by the chefs in San Sebastian who did a similar thing for Spanish cuisine in the 70s, but also Danish film-makers like Lars von Trier, who in the mid-90s had invented Dogme, a pared-down, purist school of Danish cinema.

"I was very inspired by the Dogme brothers," says Meyer. "I thought if they could do it, then we could also do it."

With a background in business, Meyer then came up with a long-term plan to revitalise Danish food that addressed different aspects of the food business: farmers, wholesalers like Arla, consumers and also politicians. But first he realised he needed to win over other Danish chefs (many of whom were continentally minded, and had mocked his and Redzepi's regional ambitions at Noma) because it was they who could most easily influence the public's food habits.

"Society needed chefs to act as role-models," says Meyer. "We didn't need chefs to be like Gordon Ramsay. We needed chefs to be responsible people who would inspire the whole population to redefine their eating habits and their relationship to Mother Earth."

Meyer felt that government-led initiatives that used pamphlets and adverts to change how people ate were counterproductive. Instead, he wondered: "What would happen if the top chefs in our region stood up and said they were going to change things?" Trying to answer that question, he invited leading chefs and critics from all over Scandinavia to a two-day symposium in Copenhagen. Eighteen hours later, the assembled group had hammered out a ten-point plan that set out the aims and goals of the movement. It begins: "The aims of New Nordic Cuisine are: 1. To express the purity, freshness, simplicity and ethics we wish to associate with our region. 2. To reflect the changing of the seasons in the meals we make. 3. To base our cooking on ingredients and produce whose characteristics are particularly excellent in our climates, landscapes and waters." A movement was born.

Bi Skaarup was there. "I was very inspired by it," she says. "But inside I was thinking: 'Yes, Claus, this is a very

Rene Redzepi & Claus Meyer: pioneers of the New Nordic kitchen

beautiful dream. But let's see if it succeeds.' And it has. Not in my wildest dreams would I have dared think it would do so well." One of Skaarup's fears was that Meyer and Redzepi were trying to stand up for too large an area. "In the speech he gave, Claus said: 'We're now going to create a new Nordic kitchen.' And that's completely crazy because you can't make one kitchen. It's farther from Copenhagen to the north of Norway than it is from Copenhagen to the Sahara." But in the end, her fear has proved unfounded because the New Nordic kitchen is less about creating one recipe book for the entire region and more about spreading a shared set of values. It's about people, wherever they are, cooking whatever food is local and seasonal to them.

It's also about spreading ideas and know-how. The tenth

and last point in the manifesto speaks of a desire "to join forces… for the benefit and advantage of everyone in the Nordic countries". This includes not just chefs joining forces with farmers and retailers, but chefs joining forces with each other. Traditionally, the recipe for a restaurant's signature dish has been a closely guarded secret known only by the head chef and a few trusted assistants. But the New Nordic chefs try to share recipes and ideas in the hope that they'll all eventually benefit – and nowhere is that concept clearer than on Lars Williams' Nordic Food Lab, gently bobbing in the waves outside Noma.

"Hey, Chef!" says Williams to a dark-haired man breezing through the houseboat on his way to the restaurant. It's Redzepi himself, too busy for an interview, but relaxed enough to sing along to the jazz playing on the stereo. "Ba-ba-bala-lala," he sings, and waltzes out the door – the first and last I'll see of him. Williams sees him rather more, and since my visit has moved to a more formal role at Noma itself. But he stresses that the lab – founded by Redzepi and Meyer in 2008 – is not merely an extension of the restaurant next door. "Our research is for Scandinavia in general," he explains, in a voice so quiet that it's later hard to hear what he says on my dictaphone. "We want to be an inspiration to all chefs and restaurants." It's early days, and he admits that disseminating his ideas is hard. But some of his concoctions have already been adopted by the chefs at Relæ; he's preparing a Copenhagen-themed garum (or fish sauce) for local fishermen to make from their catches in the city's harbour;

he regularly holds workshops for chefs, and writes about his progress and recipes on the lab's website. His two colleagues – one a culinary anthropologist, the other a scientist – also feed their research at the lab back into university debate.

Williams didn't start out in the kitchen. At university, he studied English literature – the first 15 lines of *Paradise Lost* are tattooed on his arm – and after leaving, he art-directed music videos for Madonna. But at home, he was nevertheless "completely mental about food. I had pork legs hanging in my living room. I was always baking my own bread and playing around with home fermentation. And then I was just like: I need to do this for real." Work in New York kitchens soon followed, and a few years later he was heading up Heston Blumenthal's food laboratory at the Fat Duck in Bray. It sounds a similar job to the one he now holds, but again Williams stresses the difference. There, he was working for one man, and one restaurant. Now he's working for everyone.

Aside from developing local produce, this work currently has two themes. The first centres on finding an alternative to meat, since cattle-farming is a major contributor to global warming. The second involves experimenting with micro-organisms like yeast. "We want to create an arsenal of micro-organisms that chefs can use in the same way that they use an oven or a knife or a mixer," Williams explains. "People think, 'Oh, yeast. I can only make bread and beer with it.' But that's not entirely true."

The fried barley mould is a good example of how

Lars Williams at the Nordic Food Lab

Williams is trying to achieve both ends. As silly as it sounds, this slab of mould – comparable in size and texture to a flapjack – could replace a steak as a main course. At the same time, it's also an example of how to use micro-organisms as a kitchen appliance. Taking a sack of barley grains, he soaks and steams them for 24 hours before coating them with a fungal yeast and leaving them in a highly humid container. After a day and half, the yeast has worked its magic, so Williams removes the grains once more and before my eyes he fries them – now packed closely together like a slice of cake – in rapeseed oil.

We try some. We like it. It has a texture that I think is

somewhere between a lamb chop and a cereal bar – but what do I know? "Mmm," says Williams. "There is some sweetness, but also an umami fatness. It's almost like a honey-cured ham – but actually they're just grains that have been changed by a micro-organism."

Williams is less impressed with the mouldy sunflower seeds he has subjected to the same process. They're too oily, too fatty. "It doesn't taste amazing – and that's our criteria," says Williams. "It has to taste amazing." And if it doesn't, he says he abandons the experiment immediately. "That's the difference between this and a university laboratory. We don't have to work through everything to the nth degree."

On the bottom deck of the houseboat, we find jar after jar of equally bizarre experiments, into which Williams periodically plunges a pipette so that I can have a taste. There are pots of buckwheat and yellow peas that have been fermenting for a year. A kombucha floating in carrot juice. Oil made from local pine trees. Grasshopper garum. Quince vinegar. A very large rock. What does that do? I ask. "Oh, that's just a rock," smiles Williams. "We're not fermenting the rock. Not yet." But he could be on the verge of something similarly unexpected: a Danish curry.

"Denmark isn't really known for spice," says Williams, "so we wondered if there were ways of making our own." It was a process of trial and error – but eventually he discovered that if you dried slices of Danish cucumber at 60 degrees, then ground down the desiccated slivers, you ended up with a reddish powder that tastes first sweet, then salty, then peppery – and finally like a spice.

It's pretty high-end stuff – and 20 years ago the suggestion that anything as highfalutin as this would be happening here in the harbour of Copenhagen would have seemed laughable. When Bent Christensen wrote to the Michelin guide in the late 70s to ask if they might cover a few Danish restaurants, Michelin replied saying they doubted there were any restaurants of note in Denmark.

"Danish food culture was really down the pan," remembers Bi Skaarup, at home on her farm in Falster, southern Denmark, where she hosts courses about the history of Danish food. "If mother had an evening off, you had pizza, Coca Cola, and chips."

Copenhagen's top restaurants looked to Paris for their inspiration, while Danish bread – once proudly varied – became limited to a few different kinds of loaves. "We once had more bakers than you did in Britain," says Skaarup. "Even in the smallest villages, there would be a baker. But during the 70s and 80s, they started getting a lot of competition from the supermarkets, who were creating things that were much, much cheaper. At the same time, this fashion of eating white bread became more and more common."

Rye bread became comparatively less fashionable – particularly sad for a country where rye has been a strong part of the food culture. Behind Skaarup, the flat Danish fields scud towards the sea, punctured only by the occasional windmill. "The northern border for growing wheat goes straight through here. South of here you could grow wheat.

North of here, you couldn't. I usually say it's right through our farm."

It wasn't always like this. Towards the end of the 19th century, rye bread consumption was at its height, thanks to the very Danish invention of *smørrebrød* – otherwise known as open sandwiches. A nascent bourgeoisie had emerged in Copenhagen. For the first time, large numbers of people had disposable income – and so they started eating out more. High-end restaurants opened, and in order to compete with the new businesses, the traditional wine and beer cellars realised they had to up their game. So they took the bland food they had always sold – rye bread and butter – and began to layer it with more exotic delicacies.

"First, they would have lobster, Russian caviar," says Skaarup. "But it was actually the smørrebrød that used the old Danish recipes – frikadeller [meatballs], salted beef, 'exploded ox', pickled herring, the usual peasant food – that became most popular. And it saved the rye bread. At that point, wheat had suddenly become very cheap – but because it was fashionable to eat *smørrebrød*, the bourgeoisie continued to eat rye."

Yet by then the wider decline in Danish food had already started – and, like many things in contemporary Denmark, it can be traced to the rise of the farming cooperatives in the late 1800s. Until that point, dairy farmers tended do everything on an individual, low-tech basis. Each farmer would milk their own cows, put the raw milk in a container and wait a couple of days until the fat had surfaced – at which point they'd skim the milk. At this stage, they were in a position to make their own individual brand of butter. On the plus side, this meant that there was a great deal of variety in Danish dairy products, and a great deal of expertise and interest in food production. However, it also meant that the food being produced was of a variable quality, and consequently unsuitable for export.

Following a disastrous harvest in the early 1890s, and with the simultaneous rise of the collective ideals explored in other chapters, Danish farmers realised they needed to do more to work together. So small groups of them formed co-operatives and clubbed together to buy the latest dairy technology. These machines could quickly generate large quantities of skimmed milk and cream that were all of a high standard – and which enabled the farmers to create cheeses and butters that were at last suitable for the export market. Over the course of the 20th century, these cooperatives grew larger and larger through mergers – and by the 1950s and 60s, there were only a few large companies left. Similar transitions occurred in the slaughterhouses of the bacon industry.

The process was great for the Danish economy, but it also caused three problems. It eradicated much of the diversity in Danish food; it made rural communities much less engaged with their products; and because the best stuff was being sent overseas, it made the consumer less conscious of what was good cheese and what wasn't.

"We were taught in schools that we produced some of

the best agricultural products in the world – but it wasn't true," says Skaarup. "I realised I could get much better butter in Ireland, for instance, or in France. We were just very good at producing it in large amounts. And in the battle to get things sold to England, the Danish consumer lost the knowledge of what was good. At the same time, the people at the farms lost knowledge of the product. They didn't know how a great cabbage should look because they didn't grow it themselves. And at some point, they stopped slaughtering their own animals."

Simultaneously, amateur cooks were losing their sense of adventure – a change Skaarup attributes to the Danes' collective loss of confidence following the defeat to Germany in 1864. "Our pride was really broken there. We started listening to the authorities much more, instead of creating our own opinions about things – and this was also mirrored in the kitchen. Housewife associations travelled the country teaching women how to make 'correct' food. They were discouraged from being creative and fun in the kitchen."

She shows me some Danish cookbooks from the late-19th and early-20th centuries. "Look at her face!" says Skaarup, pointing at a miserable-looking woman in one photograph. "She's not having fun. These women stand in a special way. They hold the meat in a special way. It looks like it's been dipped in chlorine. There's no fun, there's no creativity any more." By the 60s, with more and more women in work, home-cooking was a thing of the past – and so was an interest in Danish cuisine.

How things have changed – although people can't agree exactly why that change happened, or when. The conventional answer is 2004, with the creation of the New Nordic manifesto, but really the seeds were sown long before then. Bi Skaarup charts it to November 1995, when three government ministers held a conference at Humlebaek's Louisiana Gallery to discuss the problem with dozens of chefs and food critics. But Bent Christensen has another suggestion: the late 70s, when a Danish chef called Erwin Lauterbach moved to Sweden. At the time, the Swedish government gave pensioners meal tickets to use at participating restaurants. The pensioners provided a lot of business, and so competition between these restaurants was fierce. Each chef had to be particularly inventive in order to win the pensioners' support.

"To make money, Lauterbach had to be very creative. He learned to make celery in 15 ways. He used special fish, special parts of the cow, special parts of the pig – like the nose, or ear or tail. Fish of no reputation. Vegetables of no reputation. And he had to focus on local produce, because it had to be cheap. So he invented simple Nordic cooking, because he started to be creative with local foods that people did not think were normally eatable. He was the one starting the tradition."

But it would not be fair to end this account without devoting more space to Claus Meyer, the man who founded Noma, and who asked Rene Redzepi to work there in the first place. Outside Denmark, Meyer is virtually unknown, and it is Redzepi who gets all the publicity. But while Redzepi deserves the adulation he receives, his success is mostly in making Noma what it is today. Meyer's role has been far wider: he has had a hand in virtually every area of the Danish food resurgence.

Early in the chapter, I mentioned that the story of Danish cuisine is about more than one man and, as Skaarup's and Christensen's different narratives show, there are many people and influences in play here. But Claus Meyer deserves a special place in the pantheon, because few people have understood as well as him how Danish food could be saved. He realised early on that the problem could not be solved simply through individual restaurants. It was about whole-sale social change.

Some chefs look down on Meyer because he has never run a gourmet kitchen himself. But he has done virtually everything else. He's published 14 cookbooks and hosted his own show – *Meyer's Kitchen* – on Danish television for the past two decades. Aside from Noma, Meyer has founded three other restaurants, each aimed at achieving New Nordic goals at more affordable prices. With Redzepi, he founded the Nordic Food Lab. He owns a bakery chain, he lectures in food science at the University of Copenhagen and runs a cooking school that teaches the values of the New Nordic cuisine. He has a catering business, a vinegar brewery and an organic orchard. He heads a research project aimed at improving children's food. He set up a series of allotments for public use. Most recently, he filmed a show where he

trained convicts to cook, a concept later used by Gordon Ramsay. In his spare moments, Meyer runs a programme that teaches underprivileged Bolivians to cook. Incidentally, as a teenager, he was a regional badminton champion.

"It is a never-ending story," he says when we meet in his garden in Frederiksberg, a smart part of Copenhagen. "My idea was to make a kind of virus, to create an enormous amount of initiatives and events and projects and partnerships that together in a very smooth, frictionless way would have an effect on both demand and supply. It was a total attack on this food culture of ours. My feeling is that it doesn't work if the government comes in with some decree.

Opening a restaurant doesn't work on its own. But if you do a lot of things together, and you try to include a lot of people, and you inspire them and you think about both those who act and those who consume, then you might get a kind of critical mass. It's like the snowball effect, or a tipping point."

In this light, though Noma is the most famous of Meyer's projects, it is but one of many means to an end. "When we started Noma, there were two objectives. One was to make a fantastic restaurant. The other was to challenge the French restaurant model, which was the way of the top restaurants in Denmark at that time. So it was just one means in my struggle to open the minds of my fellow Danes to the potential of food culture. Noma was the launch. But I wanted to do something that was much more for ordinary people. I wanted to deal with the everyday meal, the egalitarian meal. And so I had to focus on how to change demand – how to inspire consumers to be part of this thing."

Meyer ran his own chocolate business as a teenager, but it wasn't until 1983, when he was 20, that he had his culinary epiphany. With an alcoholic mother and an absentee father, Meyer felt lonely and directionless. "So I said, what the hell – let me win some time. I'll go to France. There was no real reason for it – I just went." First, he went to Paris, where he lived with a dentist and cooked for his mistresses. But then Meyer came down with hepatitis and moved to Gascony to recover. He ended up living with the family of a pastry chef called Guy.

"That family," he remembers, with some emotion, "they couldn't have children, but they'd always wanted a boy. So they treated me like their lost son and spoiled me with fantastic cakes and desserts and love. As soon as I recovered from my disease – and I did it extremely quickly, to the surprise of all the doctors – I started working with Guy, who became my spiritual father, my mentor and my muse. And in contrast to my actual father, he taught me that I was good at something and he taught me that I could do great things and that I should love what I was doing."

Something stirred. It wasn't the full-scale understanding of food culture that he has today. It was just the realisation that people weren't eating very well back home in Denmark. "I was compelled by the idea of going to a cheese shop and knowing what cheese is best at what time of year," says Meyer. "The idea of spending five hours just to prepare a meal for your family. The idea of spending three hours just to share it. And then when I came back to Denmark I saw the opposite. I saw a desert. With only one cheesemaker, one pea producer, one slaughterhouse supplying the whole nation with uniform, generic, passionless food. And I saw a people without passion and love for the meal.

"I didn't truly understand the way that our monopolistic food system had created a total lack of enthusiasm for food. It was just about me, and me being the child of divorced parents. I was in lack of love. I almost didn't see my father for four or five years, my mother became an alcoholic when they divorced, my grandma died. So I felt that there was a relation between the lack of love or care, and the terrible food in Denmark. And in France I saw the opposite – an abundance of love and generosity, and taste and smell and great meals. And you can say in some ways that when I started the Nordic cuisine movement, it was a replication of what I had lived in Gascony, 20 years before."

Can the New Nordic kitchen last? Already, there are signs that a new generation of Danish chefs want to try something slightly different. One night I eat at Relæ, a new restaurant founded by Christian Puglisi, once the sous-chef at Noma. He still has close ties to his alma mater, but he doesn't want his new project to be known as Nordic. Many of his inspirations are in fact Italian, he has a no-foraging policy, and – most blasphemously of all – Puglisi uses olive oil.

Another night in Copenhagen, I find myself sitting in a disused meat market, stabbing at a table with a Stanley knife. Eventually, I carve a hole in the surface, and underneath it I find part of my supper: a bed of herbs. Earlier, I stabbed another hole, inserted a straw and slurped up some sort of mushroom soup. Later, the waiters will hand me a kebab, and I'll go outside to fry it on a barbecue with the dozen other diners. This extraordinary experience is known as "I'm A Kombo", and it's just one of the many wacky culinary concepts currently sprouting in Copenhagen. An occasional supper club rather than a permanent restaurant, "I'm A Kombo" is held twice a month by two young chefs, Lasse Askov and Bo Lindegaard, a big man with the beard of

Hagrid and the round glasses of Harry Potter. In one sense, it's the perfect example of the kind of inventiveness that the New Nordic cuisine has encouraged. The bed of herbs is the kind of thing you might find at Noma. Then again, other bits of the menu display a frustration with some of the New Nordic mantra. Each course has a theme, and the third one – with a recipe nicked from a Japanese chef – centres on theft. It's a vague dig at the way many of the New Nordic restaurants have become quite derivative and often steal each other's ideas; carrots served in a pot of earth, for instance, is now quite a hackneyed Nordic trope. Then there's the sixth course – a large chunk of malted pork that the chefs have simply called "Comfort Food". New Nordic restaurants tend to serve lots of tiny, delicate courses that aren't in themselves particularly filling, so the inclusion of something as big and homely as the pork is almost rebellious. "It doesn't really seem like it," says Lindegaard, "but we feel that it's one of the most progressive things that we do."

Lindegaard is grateful for the platform the New Nordic kitchen has given I'm A Kombo, but says it's not a movement he aspires to join. "We're definitely more international," he explains. "It would be stupid for a company like us to hook up with New Nordic cuisine. That would be the death of our future. That would be the worst business plan ever. Nordic cuisine is like the Spanish cuisine [a reference to the restaurant El Bulli, which closed recently]. It will die. Very soon. A few years ago everyone was looking at Spain.

Now everyone is looking at Copenhagen. In a few years time they will look somewhere else. So why would you want to build your business around it? I don't get it." When I put it to Meyer that the New Nordic kitchen might soon come to an end, he's phlegmatic. "Whether it will last or not last - who cares? If you're the minister responsible for tourism, then you might be worried about that. But I don't wake up in the morning and think about whether it will last."

In fact, he would welcome other regions picking up where Denmark has left off. For what's important to Meyer is the survival not of the New Nordic brand itself, but the values and solutions that come hand in hand with it. "Obesity, diabetes, healthiness, the environment, biodiversity, the empowerment of the farmer" – these are the things the New Nordic diet addresses, he says, and these are things that will last.

"It goes beyond that one restaurant," says Meyer. "It goes beyond being quoted in *Time* magazine. It's about leaving something great for the world to come after you. Maybe all the international food magazines will stop writing about New Nordic food in three or four years. I hope that maybe it will be some South American country that will prosper. Or that Greece will fight back with Albania and Romania. As a foodie I would love that. As a global citizen I would love that. It's not a war of ratings. We're not declaring war against Mexican food. It's not warfare – it's a choir. It's a global choir."

3. MORE THAN JUST CHAIRS:
the Danish design DNA

"We've had our share of chairs now... We've had our share of furniture." – Jacob Fruensgaard Øe

"I am Mr Egg," smiles a chap who turns out to be called Mr Hans Mannerhagen. You can see where he's coming from, though. The man is surrounded by dozens of cone-shaped chairs, most of which he helped build, and each one looks like half a hollowed-out hard-boiled egg. It's a slightly unworldly scene. A warm fug of leather hugs the air, while dozens of upturned domes are heaped on the ground. Some are beige, some brown, and some checked – and they're all splattered at jaunty angles across a factory floor.

The floor belongs to Fritz Hansen, one of Denmark's oldest and most famous furniture-makers, and at its centre stands Mannerhagen, the firm's master upholsterer. It's his job to fix a coat of leather to each chair's foam shell – a job that might take three days and more than 1200 stitches. Mannerhagen is almost teary at the thought. He points at a chair. "When you work on these kinds of things," he says, "you put so much of yourself in it. Your whole heart, and your whole soul. It becomes a part of me. The design. The handicraft. The history."

For these are not just any egg-shaped chairs. These are the Egg chairs, and they have been built here continuously by Fritz Hansen for the past 50 years. Along with a lot of Danish furniture from the middle of the last century, you can argue that they have almost as firm a place in Denmark's

The Egg chair – a late, lauded example of Danish Modern

recent identity as they do in the man who stitches them together. Dreamt up by the Danish architect and semi-deity Arne Jacobsen, the Eggs are a late, lauded example of Danish Modern, a school of furniture design that gripped the creative world in the 40s, 50s and 60s, and which still casts a long shadow over contemporary Danish culture. In 1951, when the UN wanted an extra debating chamber, they chose the great Danish Modernist Finn Juhl to design its interior. In 1960, when Kennedy and Nixon clashed in America's first televised presidential debate, JFK was sitting on a chair – The Chair, to give it its usual title – designed by Juhl's contemporary, Hans Wegner. In 1963, when Lewis Morley photographed a nude Christine Keeler, he asked her to sit astride a copy of another Jacobsen creation – the 7 Chair. And in 1968, when Stanley Kubrick wanted to stock the spaceship in *2001: A Space Odyssey*, he chose some of Jacobsen's cutlery.

You would recognise Danish Modern if you saw it in a sitting room. Most Danish Modern chairs are wooden ones – rich and wholesome in colour; clean and functional in their design. "In Danish and Scandinavian design," says Nille Juul-Sørensen, designer of the Copenhagen metro stations, and now head of the Danish Design Centre, "if it's not functional, we think: why the hell should we have it?"

In this respect, the leather-clad Egg is almost frivolous in comparison with its wooden, straight-faced forebears. The Egg would not have been out of place on Kubrick's spacecraft, but Wegner's The Chair – with its thin, gently rounded back and its four functional legs – is more at home at a kitchen table, or even in a classroom. But Danish Modern was about more than specific chairs – and about more than just furniture, in fact. At its most idealistic, it aimed to make Danish homes better places to live in – and the chairs were just one means of doing that.

"Last Sunday a Danish paper wrote about this 'world-famous Danish furniture designer Arne Jacobsen'," says an irritated Juul-Sørensen, a bulky man with thick 50s-style glasses. "I thought: should I take the phone and call this stupid journalist? Because Arne Jacobsen was not a furniture designer. He was an architect. And he used architecture to influence a new family life." In the fifth-storey window behind Juul-Sørensen, you can see the Tivoli Gardens, the world's most tasteful theme park. As he talks, a rollercoaster plunges groundwards. "At the time, the furniture we had was from a different decade. It was not for modern life. So Jacobsen just redesigned things to fit the new architecture, to fit the new lifestyle. And he needed some chairs [to do that]. He was not a furniture designer; he changed architecture, he changed the way we live."

Jacobsen was not the father of the movement, however; if anything, he was considered something of a rebel. Kaare Klint, the founder of the furniture department at the Danish Royal Academy, was the man who pioneered Danish Modernism in the 20s. Klint and his contemporaries were inspired by the humanist aims of the Bauhaus movement in Germany, but they felt that Bauhaus buildings and Bauhaus furniture designs were in practice not particularly humanising. Danish Modern was partly an attempt to do what the Bauhaus hadn't.

Like most of his contemporaries, Klint had a keen eye for detail. In the 30s, goes the myth, Klint was introduced to the Swedish architect Gunnar Asplund. They talked shop. "What are you working on?" Klint asked.

"Oh, just a school, a hotel and a few houses. What about you?"

"I am working on a chair," said Klint.

A few years went by before Klint and Asplund ran into each other again. "What are you working on?" Klint asked for the second time. "Oh, a town hall or two," replied Asplund. "And a couple of villas. What about you?"

"I told you last time," said Klint. "I am working on a chair."

This anecdote, told best by Andrew Hollingsworth in his book, *Danish Modern*, highlights another of the movement's tropes: painstaking craftsmanship. Their furniture was planned in excruciating detail, and was designed to last. Jill, the Fritz Hansen PR, has another way of demonstrating this. Taking a 7 Chair from its display, she places it upside down on the floor, takes off her heels and carefully steps onto the chair's back. Then she bounces, gingerly. Nothing snaps. "See!" she says, in triumph. "That's how you know it's not a fake."

Ironically, it was this emphasis on quality that killed the movement. By the end of the 60s, says Hollingsworth, con-

Hans Wegner's The Chair

sumers increasingly preferred the brash colours of pop art to the understated Danish aesthetic. Meanwhile, the Danes' careful craftsmanship could not compete with the mass-produced and mass-marketed pieces made overseas, and in 1966 the Annual Exhibition of Cabinetmakers – for decades a showcase of the best Danish design – folded. In some respects, the decline was partly due to the success of the Danish welfare state. New social legislation – including the introduction of the minimum wage – meant that the cost of labour rose dramatically, which in turn made labour-intensive industries like manufacturing increasingly unprofitable. The manufacturers that remained – like Fritz Hansen and Rud Rasmussen – had to up their prices tenfold, and started to stick to the designers they knew and trusted, rather than develop younger ones.

If you entered many Danes' homes today, you would not necessarily realise all this. To put it very glibly, if an Englishman's home is his castle, the Dane's home is her temple to the descendants of Kaare Klint. The icons of the 50s and 60s still form the centrepieces of many Danish living rooms, which helps explain why *The Bridge*'s Martin Rohde has a house full of so many design classics. I lost count of the number of houses that have a Poul Henningsen artichoke lamp hanging from the ceiling – something that regular viewers of the political drama *Borgen* (which fea-

Poul Henningsen's ubiquitous artichoke lamp

tures several Henningsens) may recognise. After an interview, a university professor proudly shows me his two prized Børge Mogensen armchairs. At a party in Vesterbro, a geography student in his late twenties says he has just saved up the equivalent of £500 to buy a Jacobsen original.

"A very high percentage of the Danes know about Arne Jacobsen," says Kristian Byrge, who runs Muuto, a thrusting new furniture company aimed at promoting younger designers. "That's one of the differences between Denmark and a lot of other countries. We are proud of our design heritage. A lot of people will own his 7 Chair. They might have bought it reduced and repainted it or reworked it, but most people buy an original. It's something we like our country to be associated with. Design is in our cultural DNA."

Speaking of Danish DNA, it is hard to continue this discussion about people's homes without mentioning the very Danish concept of *hygge*. Pronounced roughly "hoo-guh", *hygge* does not have a direct equivalent in English. It refers to the warm state of relaxation in which Danes find themselves when they're sitting around a fire with friends, or having a beer in their beach house (another Danish mainstay) on the North Sea in the summer. It is often loosely translated as "cosiness", but this seems both too broad and yet too specific a translation. When I first arrived in Denmark, I was surprised to hear many people describe all sorts of things as "cosy". My bike was cosy, their table was cosy, and so too was a walk through Vesterbro. It was slightly perplexing – until I realised my friends were substituting the adjectival form of *hygge* (*hyggelig*, or "hoogalee") for the English word "cosy". Obviously, it doesn't translate particularly well, rendering the concept less intelligible to an English ear.

Still, it's safe to say that the attainment of this homely *hygge* (whatever it is exactly) is a constant goal for Danes. In turn, this might help explain both why Denmark has the second-largest homes in Europe (in terms of square metres per capita), and why the Danes are so concerned with making those homes look nice. Since restaurants are so expensive (thanks to a 25% tax on food), many Danes prefer to spend their evenings at home. Interior design is therefore incredibly important, and so too is Arne Jacobsen.

But therein lies a problem. A fixation on past masters is stifling the designers of today. "When you talk Danish design outside Denmark, people believe it's an old chair," says Juul-Sørensen, who says he took on his new job in order to challenge that perception. He has an uphill battle, if the exhibits at the Danish Design Museum, a few kilmetres north-east of Juul-Sørensen's Danish Design Centre, are anything to go by. The fixation with chairs reaches almost comical levels here. As if in a furniture mausoleum, visitors to the museum process past a serpentine line of chairs that never seems to end. Chair after chair after chair; it is like an eery, empty, hyper-extended doctor's waiting room. "We call it Danish Modern," laments Juul-Sørensen, "but Danish Modern was actually designed in the 50s and 60s. People don't realise that we are now doing a lot of other stuff."

Thing is, much of that other stuff struggles to get made. Fritz Hansen only release one new piece of furniture a year, and even these ranges tend to be – by their own admission – influenced by the dead designers already in their collection.

"If you were a designer ten years ago," claims Juul-Sørensen, "you didn't have a future. A lot of these young designers could not get a job as a chair designer because when they went to Fritz Hansen and said, "Look I have designed this new funky chair," [Fritz Hansen] would say: "It looks cool, but we have a chair designed in the 50s which sells nine million pieces [a year], so no, not interested." So these companies squeezed out a whole generation."

Thomas Bentzen, one of the few designers from that era who did make it, remembers the frustration well. "It was like: 'I've got this table and it's made completely out of metal and it has this handle so you can move it around. Which Danish company do I want to approach with this? Who would see the good design potential in this table?' And I'm not sure any of the classic Danish companies would have seen that."

In Denmark, people are finally making new furniture, but in the main it is produced by young firms like Hay, Gubi, Mater and the aforementioned Muuto – companies set up in the last few years to promote young Danish designers, and to challenge the creative hegemony established by the likes of Fritz Hansen. In fact, some of their most well-known work is a very obvious piss-take of the classics. Hay's Nobody Chair is made entirely from fabric, which is a dig at Danish Modern's obsession with wood – while its very name mocks how the Danish tradition has become so focussed on the identity of individual designers, rather than the ideas they originally stood for. Meanwhile, Muuto's Rest – a sofa without a strongly defined shape – is a deliberate contrast to the more rigid structures you might find at Fritz Hansen.

This isn't a criticism of the old furniture firms. The direction they have taken is simply sound business sense, and the work they make is still beautiful. It's just that they no longer have the same innovative spark that made them so important and exciting in the middle of the last century. This isn't only because they don't promote many new designers; they also lack the same democratic values they had in the 50s.

Most of the Danish Modernists did not just want to make good furniture; they wanted to make good furniture that everyone could enjoy. They aspired to make better homes for the masses – and they could do this only if their furniture was both well-made and affordable. This meant that many of the pieces now sold as expensive classics were, 50 years ago, well within the reach of the average Dane. Today, Jacobsen's 7 Chair costs around £250. When it was first released, the chair cost ten times less. Hans Wegner's Children's Chair is now priced at around £70; once it was a tenner. Wegner was one of several designers who made furniture for FDB, a large chain of cooperative supermarkets. Headed by another Danish Modern icon, Børge Mogensen, FDB's design department was like a proto-IKEA – except that, unlike the contemporary Swedish firm, the furniture FDB made was not only affordable; it was of an unparalleled quality.

The Danish Modernists also wanted their furniture to change the way people lived at home. This meant that most were less interested in their furniture as a set-piece, and more concerned with the context in which it was placed and the domestic problems it could help solve. Mogensen spent a decade analysing how Danes used shelves and storage space. He worked out the kinds of objects the average Dane possessed and then calculated how much space each object required. The result was the Øresund shelf range, developed between 1955 and 1967, which had the commendable, if lofty, ambition of solving every domestic storage problem with which Danes might be presented.

Like many democratic concepts in Denmark, this progressive design culture was not a sudden invention. "It came out of that whole folk high school, co-op way of thinking," explains Thomas Dickson, author of a large tome with a fairly self-explanatory title: *Dansk Design*. "A lot of architects joined something called the Architect Help. They designed blueprints for farmhouses, schools, tenement buildings – and they gave them away for free. Anyone could get a copy. If you needed to build a farmhouse, you could get a blueprint for just the cost of the print."

Schools were designed by respected architects; old people's homes were furnished by designers. "And that process of giving stuff away for free," adds Dickson, whose office chair is incidentally a version of The Chair by Hans Wegner, "came out of the concept of sharing farm resources." This meant that by the time the 30s arrived, a generation of Danes had grown up surrounded by – and with an appreciation for – good design, while a generation of designers had grown up understanding the need to make that design available to all.

It is this egalitarian legacy that Denmark's old-school furniture-makers have now partly lost. While researching this book, I became obsessed with finding where that legacy might now be. At first, it made sense to look for it in the offices of young furniture firms like Muuto, Mater and Hay. Of these, Muuto have made the most visible attempt to position themselves as a new direction in Danish design – their slogan is "New Nordic Design" – and so it was there that I headed first.

Once I arrive, what surprises me is how this tagline is in fact more a branding exercise than a manifesto for a new design movement. They are new Nordic, rather than new Danish, for a reason: they don't want to be tied down to one country, one set of values, or for their pieces to have a recognisable aesthetic. Tellingly, Muuto represent designers not just from Denmark, but from across Scandinavia – and even then they would prefer to be seen as international players, rather than from a particular region. The triple concepts of affordability, simplicity, and attention to detail – standard throughout Scandinavian design – are still central to them, but in aesthetic terms, they'd rather not be seen as simply Scandinavian, or even simply Muuto.

"At Muuto, we try to make stuff that is not all the same kind of design," says the firm's co-founder Kristian Byrge, who perhaps unsurprisingly, given his nose for a good slogan, has a background in business rather than furniture. "It has a variation in materials, and in looks. So you can actually put our work together in a home and you don't feel like it's a Muuto home."

One of Muuto's most prominent pieces is the Around, a coffee table by Thomas Bentzen. You can see it on sale at big museums like Humlebaek's Louisiana Gallery – a simple, squat, three-legged disc, coated in block colours and ringed with a tall rim that does not quite stretch around the table's entire circumference. Trying to work out what it is to be a furniture designer in the post-Jacobsen era, I ask Bentzen to take me through the process that led him to create it.

It emerges that the table's only distinctive feature – the rim with the gap in it – is both inspired by the rimmed coffee tables of the Danish Modern period, and necessitated by the flaws of contemporary manufacturing.

"Looking back at my childhood," says Bentzen, a tall, bald, softly spoken Dane, "the coffee tables I used to love often had an edge, and so I knew that I wanted to work with one."

In the old days, though, that edge would have been

carved by hand from a solid block of wood. Today, this process would be too costly and too lengthy – so Bentzen's rim actually comes from a separate piece of wood, and is stuck to the rest of the table with glue. And the difficulty with this method is that the glued rim cannot stretch all the way around the table – hence the gap.

I like the table, and Bentzen's explanation makes it clear how a contemporary furniture designer might be inspired by Danish Modern, and yet diverge from it. But something doesn't quite add up – and eventually I realise it's because we've spent ten minutes talking about what a table looks like, rather than how that table might help shape people's behaviour. In aesthetic terms, I understand how the table relates to Danish Modern – but, like the beautiful work at Fritz Hansen, I can't work out how it channels the movement's sense of democratic design. Sure, it's affordable – but it's not as cheap as IKEA. Sure, it's good quality, and good-looking, and it's even made by the same cooperative – FDB – who made Danish Modern ranges for the masses in the 50s. But there's the rub: it's not solving domestic problems like Børge Mogensen's shelves aimed to. It's being sold to tourists at Denmark's biggest art galleries. I like Muuto, and I like their work. But I came here in search of Danish Modernism's spiritual successors, and I am not sure these are them.

Again, this isn't a criticism. It's just an acknowledgement that furniture design can no longer have the same social impact that it at least aimed to have in the 50s. Of course, design doesn't have to change the world to be beautiful. As Peter Bundgaard Rützou – the co-creator of another contemporary classic: the stool you can find in one of Denmark's largest bakery chains – points out: "This whole discussion about the role of the designer, it's great. But you still need a chair to sit on. And I like the fact a chair is THERE. I like the fact it's physically there. So even though I like the ideas behind, say, interaction design, and the way it addresses what kind of society we live in, I find more personal pleasure in this stuff."

You can't really argue with that. But at the same time, it's interesting that Bundgaard Rützou implicitly acknowledges that furniture design no longer "addresses what kind of society we live in". To find the people who today best channel the democratic values of Danish Modern, you probably need to look elsewhere.

It turns out that this is also one of Dickson's biggest bugbears. "A lot of the design made today is made in a tradition that is 40 years old," he argues. "A lot of these young furniture and lightning designers still live in this dream of being the new Hans Wegner or Arne Jacobsen. And I think they're barking up the wrong tree. If they want to design furniture they need to understand that we don't need the same kind of furniture and objects that we used to need. We have different lives than our parents and grandparents had. But I see a lot of young designers designing what are basically sculptures, large heavy chairs that you walk around like you'd walk around a Henry Moore sculpture. But most of us don't need this at home. We want to easily convert a piece of furniture into a bed, so that if we have guests, they can have a place to sleep."

Dickson says his view is unpopular with traditional designers – but he has a lively ally in Juul-Sørensen, who praises firms like Muuto and Hay, but thinks there's more to design than furniture.

"If Arne Jacobsen was around today, he would not design chairs," claims Juul-Sørensen. "We don't want any more chairs. Why the hell should we produce more chairs? I mean, there are enough chairs, everyone is pumping out chairs. These things which have no meaning in the society we are moving into."

Like Dickson, Juul-Sørensen thinks the future of interior design is in creating things that have more than one use – but his ideas are slightly more zany. "Could we actually design a dishwasher that is also an oven?" he asks. "Why isn't a washing machine a games console?" It's not such a far-fetched idea, Juul-Sørensen argues. A Playstation that only worked if you filled it with clothes might encourage children to wash more.

He may sound slightly flippant – but Juul-Sørensen has a serious point. The most progressive designers working in Denmark today are the ones who recognise that the world faces different problems from the ones it did in the 50s. They're the people creating wind turbines for Vestas, the world's leading windmill company. They're the architects at 3XN researching how to build offices out of biomass, or the

NovoNordisk engineers who revolutionised the treatment of diabetics with the pre-filled insulin syringe. Nowadays, says Dickson, they might not even be designing physical objects. "They might be more problem-orientated than object-orientated," he says. "They recognise that solving a problem might not lead to designing an object, but a solution. A service or communication or procedure."

One such group is Hatch and Bloom, founded five years ago by four young designers in Aarhus. They're not nearly as big as Denmark's most famous solutions-based firm, DesignIt, but their work is just as interesting: much of it centres on trying to solve problems within the infrastructure of Denmark's welfare state. Most recently, they were asked to help Randers Hospital improve its care of what were then called "complex" patients – people who suffered from both a medical problem, and a surgical one, like a diabetic with a broken leg. Their treatment was considered too costly and lengthy, and so Hatch and Bloom spent time analysing the hospital to find out what processes could be made better. "Eventually we realised: this is not about the patients," remembers Jacob Fruensgaard Øe, one of the firm's founders. "It's about the hospital. The patient isn't complex. The hospital is."

Hatch and Bloom discovered that though many surgical specialists were at the top of their game, they seemed to have forgotten over the course of their career how to deal with medical issues – and vice versa. So the designers worked out ways to integrate the different disciplines, most of them conceptual rather than physical. Some suggestions focussed on changing the way doctors perceived complex patients.

"One night we snuck into the hospital," says Fruensgaard Øe. "We had these little posters. And we posted them on everything, from toilet paper to uniforms to parking lots and water glasses. The posters said: 'only for medical staff'; 'only for surgical staff'. We did it as a stunt. To make them look at their culture and realise that this hospital apartheid is not good for anyone."

Other ideas were more practical. Hatch and Bloom suggested that rather than splitting the care of a complex patient between different departments, they should be placed in a special ward devoted to complex treatment, where specific doctors and nurses should coordinate all aspects of their recovery. Ideas-based consultancy like this is often mocked, but in this case, it had results: treatment times for complex patients (now called cross-patients after another Hatch and Bloom suggestion) is down by a fifth. Though they barely work with physical objects, Fruensgaard Øe thinks his firm is among the worthiest inheritors of the Danish design tradition. "Fifty years ago, these chairs changed something. But we can't do that again. We've had our share of chairs now. We've had our share of furniture. What we're doing – the immaterial, service part – is what, when people look back in 50, 70 years, will be talked about."

Whether this is true remains to be seen, but it's certainly the way things are going at the moment. Traditionally,

Denmark's top design school has been at the Royal Academy in Copenhagen – but the one most people are talking about these days is in a small provincial town in Jutland. With no furniture department and a focus on industrial and interactive design, you could argue the rise of Kolding Design school mirrors that of Denmark. Even ten years ago, Kolding was still very focussed on what things looked like.

"Aesthetics, aesthetics, aesthetics," says the eccentric Barnabas Wetton, an expat Brit, a former BBC reporter, and now a director of studies in interaction design at Kolding. "Aesthetics. We were very good at aesthetics. All around us, society was changing so rapidly – yet I could only see students who could make nice things, but weren't very effective." In 2003, the school made its first trip to China – and it was there that he says they realised "that people became better and fuller and happier designers when they understood they were working for others and not just for themselves, and that they were able to provide real value to society."

It sparked a sea change at Kolding, and a decade later they have an international reputation for interaction design. Their approach is not exactly unique, but it is more successful than many. According to Wetton, the school and its affiliates have exhibited six times at New York's Museum of Modern Art – more than any other education institution in Europe.

At Kolding, design is now taught "as a social practice; design as a way of organising the way that we act in societies." One of his PhD students, Eva Knutz, is analysing how to use computer games to get hospitalised children to express their feelings – emotional design, she calls it – while another unionised the Danish modelling industry.

These projects may sound slightly vague, or at least very removed from conventional perceptions of design. But Wetton's is the most convincing explanation I've heard of how traditional Danish design ideals can be applied to the modern world.

"We have a serious problem in Europe and in the Western world. We have to reorganise our societies for the post-industrial age and for the green age. This means we have to take our societies apart and rebuild them and remake them into something else."

Kolding wants to be at the forefront of this reorganisation. To do this, the school has had to rethink exactly which practical skills it should teach its students. Their work is now as much about researching how people behave as it is about making things for them, and so the course has been restructured accordingly.

"There's a whole series of techniques our students learn regardless of what field they're in," says Wetton. "Working with people, the way it is you ask questions, the way it is you glean knowledge from the situation we're designing for."

Sometimes this process takes the form of "body-storming" – like a brainstorm, but using physical rather than mental experiences to stimulate ideas. Recently, robotics researchers at the University of Southern Denmark asked a group of Kolding students to design the interface for a robot that could be used to take blood samples in Danish hospitals instead of human nurses. As part of the project's body-storm phase, every single student had to learn to take blood from real patients. "We had to understand that fear of having blood taken, to understand the process of it." What they soon realised was that patients would only stand for their arm being injected with a syringe by a robot if a) they couldn't see the injection taking place; and b) the robot looked nothing like a robot. So what they came up with instead was a cosy, dolphin-shaped armrest into which a patient would slot her arm. A hidden infrared ray would then identify the right vein, an unseen syringe would pop out momentarily, prick the skin and then shoot back into the armrest, ready for testing.

Quite why such an extraordinary robot was designed in the first place – and the implications it has for Denmark's massive welfare state – will be explored in the next chapter.

4. POOR CARINA:
the problem with the welfare state

"The welfare state we have is excellent in most ways. We only have this little problem. We can't afford it."
– Gunnar Viby Mogensen

There is a well-known sketch by a pair of Norwegian comedians in which a Dane tries to buy a bike tyre from a hardware store. Things begin badly. The man behind the counter can't understand his compatriot's accent – but is too embarrassed to say so. Instead, he just takes a wild guess at what the cyclist wants and hands over a long file. Then things get worse. It turns out the cyclist can't understand the vendor either, but is similarly too polite to admit it. So he pretends the file is what he wanted all along and asks how much it costs. The vendor tells him, but again the cyclist can't work out what was said, so he ends up holding out a fistful of Danish kroner and allows the hardware man to pluck the appropriate amount from his hands. To round off the farce, a cunning milkman enters to ask if the store needs 1000 milk bottles. Again, the vendor can't understand a word of the milkman's question, says yes simply to make things easier and is landed with one of the largest domestic grocery bills ever known in Scandinavia.

The sketch's popularity on YouTube shows how successfully it riffs on traditional Scandinavian stereotypes. The Swedes and the Norwegians think the Danes are loud, brash and unintelligible – even to each other. The Danes think the Swedes (their medieval rivals) are uptight control freaks. Both joke that the Norwegians are mere provincial bumpkins (Norway was once a colony of both Denmark and Sweden), while everyone thinks the Finns are weird. You can see a tongue-in-cheek exaggeration of these hackneyed tropes in the first episode of *The Bridge*, when a Danish detective (played by Kim Bodnia) is paired with a Swedish one (Sofia Helin) after a dead body is found draped over the two countries' mutual border. When a woman needs to drive through a crime scene to get to her husband's hospital, Bodnia – the laid-back Dane – gives her the go-ahead before Helin – the pedantic Swede – slaps him down. Later, Bodnia tries to make a joke to a group of Swedish coppers. Cue: tumbleweed. Like in the Norwegian skit, no one understands him.

These stereotypes are of course just that: stereotypes. But some of them have distant roots in truth – and in the case of the Danes, it's in the fact that their language, once very similar to Norwegian and Swedish, has developed an increasing number of blurred word endings and glottal stops. When I first tried to learn Danish, I was amazed that a language could carry as many silent consonants as English. One of the first phrases I came across was the Danish for "what about you?" Written down, it is "*Hvad med dig*?" Out loud, it sounds like more of a mush: "vamedye?" Of its seven consonants, only three are pronounced. In other phrases, "*ikke*" (the Danish word for "not") should technically be pronounced "ee-ker", but in fact sounds more like the English word "air"; the Danish "d" is often softened into a kind of "l"-sound; while the "g" is sometimes lost altogether. In a famous example, the Danish word for cake was once the same as it still is in Swedish: "*kaka*". But while the Swedish version remained fairly static, the Danish word has been eroded from "*kaka*" to "*kage*", and its pronunciation has drifted from "ka-ka" to "kay-ger", and from "kay-ger" to "kay-er", and from "kay-er" to something that sounds a bit like the English name "Kay".

This swallowing of unstressed syllables is nothing new – it was first documented in the 15th century by a touring Swedish bishop – and nor does it mean that Danish is any less sophisticated than languages like German and Russian, which are still fully inflected. (Word endings may have been strangled in Danish, but subtleties in meaning are instead conveyed by complex variations in word order.) However, harmless as it is, the process has sped up markedly in the last three decades, during which time the Norwegians and

Swedes have found Danish increasingly hard to understand. In part, this is because Scandinavians have been watching less of their neighbours' television and more of its English-language equivalents, and are therefore less exposed to the nuances of each other's languages.

But a group of linguistic researchers I meet at the University of Copenhagen have another intriguing theory: that this exponential increase is a by-product of the introduction in the 60s of state-subsidised childcare. The policy, which sees the state pay for around three-quarters of the cost of childcare for every toddler over one, has made it much easier for mothers to go back to work. Today, 74% of Danish mothers return to their jobs after having children, compared to just 55% in Britain.

According to the researchers, this progression may have had a harmless yet fascinating side effect. Icelandic, says Professor Marie Maegaard, is still the most conservative of the Nordic languages, because in Iceland many children grow up on isolated farms and talk a lot with their grandparents. But in Denmark, she points out, "Almost every Danish child goes to kindergarten from the age of one. And that will speed up any development because they don't talk so much with the older generations, who have more conservative diction."

Maegaard and her colleagues are still fleshing out the theory, but regardless of its accuracy, it still gives an intriguing insight into the impact of the thing that may define Denmark above all else: the welfare state.

The state is huge in Denmark. It spends more money, as a percentage of GDP, than any other country in Europe. It employs around 900,000 Danes – about a third of the Danish workforce – and unsurprisingly therefore provides a raft of free services to its citizens. Childcare, healthcare and state education are naturally three of them – but more surprisingly, so is university education and most of its living costs. Over-65s receive a basic state pension worth twice the UK version. Despite recent rule changes, they can still retire up to three years early (receiving £19,000 every year in the process). The unemployed receive up to 90% of what they earned when they were last in work. As described in Chapter one, the vast majority of private school fees are subsidised by the state. The minimum wage is over £11 an hour – the highest in the world – which in turn means that the gap between rich and poor, though larger than it was 20 years ago, is still the world's smallest. In fact, the state looks after its citizens so well that many people (usually right-wing politicians) claim that it is nearly impossible to find poverty in Denmark – much to the consternation of those on the left, including one MP in particular: Özlem Cekic. Who's right is still a moot point in the Danish media, largely thanks to Cekic's own cack-handed research. When challenged by her critics to find one Danish resident who was genuinely in poverty, Cekic presented a 36-year-old woman called Carina. Now sarcastically known in Danish tabloids as "Fattig Carina", or Poor Carina, she turned out to be receiving monthly benefits worth over £1600, which, once her bills were paid, left her with a disposable income of around £600.

Needless to say, this level of state subsidy can only really be supported by an immensely high tax bill. Danes pay high levels of income, council, church and healthcare tax – and can end up owing between 50 and 60 per cent of their income. There are also high levies on commodities like cars (180%), which is one reason you see few four-by-fours on the streets, while VAT is at 25%, and is applied to payments for food – which is why eating out is a rare luxury for most Danes. High taxes are still seen as a reasonably fair trade-off for the services received in return (fittingly, the Danish word for tax – "*skat*" – is also a term of affection) but the amount of tax people should pay, and the exact size of the state itself, are subjects of increasing debate. Nevertheless, almost all political parties – right and left – are supportive of at least the premise of a large, social democratic state, not least because the public views it with such sentiment and would not vote in large numbers for a party that worked against it.

When he was elected prime minister in 2001, Anders Fogh Rasmussen – the then leader of Venstre, the main centre-right party in Denmark – made his first speech as PM a rallying call for the welfare state. Earlier in his career, he had written a book trumpeting the virtues of neoliberalism and a shrunken government. But by 2001, he was elected with a manifesto that merely called for an end to tax increases, rather than tax cuts, and barely suggested trimming the state itself. "The difference between Venstre and the Social Democrats [Denmark's two main parties] has always been in foreign policy – how close should we be with NATO and the United States? – and in integration and immigration," explains Mads Brandstrup, a political correspondent for *Politiken*, Denmark's leading centre-left broadsheet. "It's been on other issues than the economy."

This is partly because the spectrum of Danish politics is, in economic terms at least, further to the left than it is in Britain. The far-right Danish People's Party – which ranks somewhere between Britain's UKIP and the BNP – may be Denmark's third-largest party, but only one party – the small and newly established Liberal Alliance – actively opposes the welfare state. And while Britain's Labour Party is as left-wing as mainstream parties get in the Commons, the Danish Folketinget houses two fairly large groups that lie to the left of the Social Democrats, Denmark's main left-wing party. First, there's the Socialist People's Party and then – even further to the left – Enhedslisten, a ragtag collection of communist, anarchist and green groups.

The media takes them seriously, too. Enhedslisten's de facto leader, Johanne Schmidt-Nielsen, regularly makes the headlines – and even Danish Rail once made her their in-train magazine's cover star. It was the Danish equivalent of plastering Salma Yaqoob – leader of Respect, Britain's only sizeable hard-left party – all over First Capital Connect. To understand why there is such consensus for a social democratic model, we need first to rewind several generations, not just to the late 19th century, and to the cooperatives and folk high schools mentioned in previous chapters, but to the late 1780s, when revolutionary fervour was sweeping most of Europe. Most, but not all. In Denmark, political change did not arrive until 1848, even though the country was subject, like France, to an absolute monarchy: the house of Oldenborg, a line of kings stretching back to the Middle Ages who were almost always called Christian or Frederick. The reason why Denmark did not yet go the way of France was that the Danish king at the end of the 18th century – Christian VII – recognised the need, out of self-preservation if nothing else, to grant his citizens greater freedom. Previously, peasants had been forbidden to leave the farms where they grew up, and instead had to work in a quasi-feudal relationship for the local landowner – a system known as adscription. In the summer of 1788, Christian VII abolished adscription, a move which paved the way for peasants to set up their own smallholdings.

The short-term impact was clear. There was no revolution, and a group of grateful farmers even erected a monument to the king on one of the approaches to Copenhagen. The long-term impact was larger. First, the state began to be seen as an enabler of freedom – as a social good rather than the authoritarian creature it is considered in many countries, perhaps even in Britain. According to the historian Daniel Levine, by the early 1900s many Danes talked about the state, society, the public and the public sector as if they were talking about the same thing. Second: the abolition of adscription turned the rural underclass into a newly aspirational breed of farmers – the very same people whose descendants would be educated in Grundtvig's folk high schools, and would then go on to found the thousands of farming cooperatives described in earlier chapters.

By the late-19th century, this new class of entrepreneurial farmers had even formed a new political party in opposition to Højre, the group of conservatives who represented the interests of the larger landowners and the urban elite. By the 1890s, this party was not just championing the cooperative movement, but also campaigning for Denmark's first pieces of social legislation: a primitive pension scheme for labourers that was introduced in 1891; social insurance (1892); and accident insurance (1898).

In the pages of the *Danish Journal of Agriculture* from the period, you can see this party's politicians make a parallel argument for both the furthering of the cooperative movement and state support of the elderly and the sick. That party's name? Venstre. Over the years, Venstre has become a party of business, and though a version of Højre still exists as the Danish Conservatives, Venstre – through its sheer size – could be described as Denmark's nearest equivalent to the Conservative party in Britain. But it is significant that Venstre, unlike the Tories, has its roots in the premise of the collective and in the battle for social equality, something which helps to explain why much of the Danish right, with their distant roots in the agrarian community, is still reluctant to take an axe to the welfare state.

Borgen: the Danish parliament

"There is a way in which the Danish welfare state," writes Knud Jespersen in his *History of Denmark*, "with its comprehensive social safety net and high level of collective responsibility, can be perceived as a modern, national version of the old village collectives from before the time of agrarian reform. These created a secure framework for the everyday life of the Danes over centuries and shaped their behaviour and norms to the point of defining what it meant to be Danish. The welfare state, with its innate security and collective protection against threats from both within and without, touched on something very deep in the heart of the Danish sense of nationality."

Indeed, when Denmark initially voted against joining the EU in 1992, it was not simply because of a knee-jerk reaction from right-wingers. A great deal of the Euroscepticism came from Danes who feared that diktats from Brussels could eventually undermine the independence of Denmark's welfare model.

Venstre is a funny name. Often translated as "the Liberal Party", it literally means "Left", which is amusing given the conservative role they now play in Danish politics. It's a hangover from the 19th century, when they were created in opposition to Højre, a party that literally meant "Right". Nor is Venstre the only odd feature of Danish political nomenclature. In the political drama *Borgen*, the fictional prime minister Birgitte Nyborg is the leader of the Moderates, a party based on the real-life Radikale Venstre. Literally translated as "the Radical Left", Radikale Venstre is in fact neither left nor radical. The result of a schism in Venstre during the early 1900s, the mild-mannered group sits slap bang in the centre of Danish politics – more socially liberal than Venstre, but too economically liberal for the Social Democrats.

The latter were the defining force of Danish politics in the 20th century, though they were locked out of power for the first decade of the 21st. Founded not long after Venstre in 1871, the Social Democrats rose to prominence in the turbulent 20s, as Denmark's finances collapsed, and the electorate grew frightened of Venstre's by now ardently capitalist approach. As in much of Europe, unemployment had rocketed, the farming industry was close to ruin, and extremist political parties were gathering momentum. Once in power, the Social Democrats attempted to fight these problems with what is now known as the Kanslergade Agreement, a huge raft of reforms agreed after much debate with the three other main parties. Signed the day Hitler took power in Germany in 1933, it formalised labour rights, introduced state support for the economy, and gave large subsidies to the farmers. It was a seismic moment, not just because it was another large step towards the Danish welfare state that was finally realised in the 70s, but because it helped solidify a nascent model for consensus-based politics in Denmark – the kind which is dramatised to such acclaim in *Borgen* and the first series of *The Killing*.

It required the agreement of the four major parties of the time, and so all four had to compromise. Conscious that a failure to reach an agreement might undermine the legitimacy of parliament and lead – eventually – to fascism, Venstre backtracked on its previous opposition to social reforms. The Social Democrats retreated from some of their more Marxist policies, and so created a politics of compromise that has been a central part of the Danish parliament ever since. No party has held absolute power for a century now, while each of the four oldest parties has, with the exception of the Conservatives and the Social Democrats, been in coalition with each of the others. This is to a large extent also due to the Danish system of proportional representation, which guarantees at least one seat to any party that wins more than 2% of the national vote, and which therefore makes it almost impossible for any party to win an overall majority. But it is also testament to the importance the Danes place on working together.

The wrangling you see in *Borgen* is apparently not that great a departure from the machinations of most recent real-life elections – with one key difference. In the real world, all the parties approach the election in two broad coalitions – one on the left and one on the right – and whichever bloc wins more than half of the Folketinget's 179 seats forms a government. The decisions about which parties will be allied to whom, who will be prime minister, and which politicians would hold which cabinet positions were their coalition to win, are all announced before the election so that the public can have the clearest idea of who they're voting for. In *Borgen*, by contrast, Birgitte Nyborg's party enters the election as the junior party in the left-wing bloc – but then performs unexpectedly well in the polls, allowing her to start new negotiations and form a new coalition after the election has taken place.

Reality followed fiction in 2011 when – a year after Nyborg was first sighted on Danish television screens – Helle Thorning-Schmidt, the leader of the Social Democrats and daughter-in-law of Labour's Neil Kinnock, was elected as Denmark's first female prime minister. It was a curious election. Unlike Nyborg, Thorning-Schmidt's left bloc does not quite have an absolute majority. Meanwhile, the Social Democrats themselves actually emerged with fewer seats than they had in opposition, something that highlighted a quirk of the Danish electoral system: a party can technically lose the election, but still form a government if their coalition partners perform strongly enough. In 2011, the parties on the extremes of the red bloc – the Radikale Venstre (RV) in the centre and Enhedslisten on the left – did unexpectedly well, which makes Thorning-Schmidt problematically reliant on the support of both. In a way, the Social Democrats were victims of their own success. The electorate knew the left bloc would probably win, so they tried to influence the direction it would take after the election by voting strongly for the parties at its fringes. A strong showing for RV would keep the coalition from going too far left, and vice versa for Enhedslisten. Unfortunately for the Social Democrats, both parties did well, which leaves Thorning-Schmidt in the political equivalent of the splits.

•

The tube I'm blowing into is unlike anything I've seen. It's connected to an iPad, and on that iPad plays a cartoon featuring an angry man who looks a little bit like Alan Sugar. Then something even stranger happens. When I stop blowing, the film stops too – and so does Sugar. Only when I start again does Sugar spring back to life. Thinking it's a coincidence, I try it all again – but then the same thing occurs. When I stop, Sugar stops. When I start, Sugar starts. Weird. And then it hits me. The iPad only works when I blow into the tube.

As unlikely as it sounds, this bizarre contraption is

actually the result of a welfare state in crisis. I'm in the robotics wing of the University of Southern Denmark in Odense – the home, incidentally, of Hans Christian Andersen. A false limb lies on a table, and all around me are prototypes for robots that could one day perform some of the tasks currently completed by humans working in state healthcare. They're all part of a project spearheaded by the university called Patient@Home – a response to the health-care challenges faced by all European countries, but which, given the size of the country's state apparatus, are particularly pronounced in Denmark. On the one hand, because the health service has fewer funds to play with, and because the population is getting older, more health professionals are retiring than can be replaced. At the same time, precisely because the population is ageing, there are more elderly people suffering from chronic disease. So there are more people to treat and fewer people to treat them – and for a country like Denmark, which prides itself on its welfare state, this is a serious problem. "In Denmark, you have the right to equal access to services no matter where you live," says Professor Anders Sørensen, one of the engineers leading the project. "That is what we as a society have decided to provide. And to be able to do that in the future, we need to make some structural changes."

According to Sørensen, some of these changes will include replacing the treatment previously provided by humans in hospitals with treatment carried out at home by robots. At first, this conjures frightening images of C-3PO running around a bathroom stabbing grannies with a syringe. But the robots Sørensen is creating are more subtle than that. As it happens, they include not just the blood-samplers whose interface was designed by the students at Kolding, but the Sugar-themed iPad described above.

At present, chronic asthma sufferers need to be treated in person, not least because the treatment is boring. If left to their own devices, a patient will often fail to complete it. But it's hoped that they could eventually treat themselves on their own at home, with the help of something incentive-based like this iPad. Since the iPad only plays movies when it is used properly, the idea is that it could coax a patient through their asthma treatment by itself, without the need for a doctor's involvement – while still allowing doctors and nurses to keep abreast of the patient's progress remotely via a digital database. This would save the patient from having to visit a hospital so often and free up hospital space for more urgent cases – particularly important in an area where nine hospitals have closed in recent years and 30% of hospital beds have been lost.

But this is about more than just healthcare. It's a symptom of a wider anxiety across Denmark; just one of many ways in which people are wondering whether, in these rocky economic times, the welfare state itself can be maintained – and if so, how.

Many people are not optimistic. When I write to the great Knud Jespersen, asking for an interview about the future of welfare, he replies mainly to explain that this will not be possible, because he is away for the spring in Switzerland. But he adds a postscript that offers some insight into what his dispirited position might have been. "I wish you a pleasant and rewarding stay in Denmark," he writes, "hopefully enjoying the setting sun over the Danish welfare state as we have known it over the last 30 years."

Few people have known that state better over the last 30 years than a venerable gentleman called Dr Gunnar Viby Mogensen. For much of his career, he was a senior researcher at the Social Research Institute, a national organ that investigates how best to improve the welfare system. More recently, he wrote one of the most comprehensive books on the subject – *The History of the Danish Welfare State since 1970* – and his conclusion about its future is, like Jespersen's, vexed. "The welfare state we have is excellent in most ways," he says, over cake and coffee in his house in Lyngby, north of Copenhagen. "We only have this little problem. We can't afford it."

Viby Mogensen cites the fact that Denmark is running a deficit worth around 3% of GDP. In global terms, particularly during a recession, this is not that high – but Viby Mogensen's concern is that it will only get bigger. Taxes cannot be raised beyond their already astronomic levels, he argues, for fear of putting off foreign business, while more Danes are emigrating for good than in previous decades, which has stunted existing tax revenues.

"This is a situation that cannot go on for ever," he claims. "We will not end up in a situation like Greece, I am sure. But we are going small steps in this direction. Which means that there is no doubt that we will have heavy welfare reforms. The only question for me is who will make these reforms. Will it be Schäuble, the German finance minister? Or will it be the Danish politicians?"

Viby Mogensen's argument is the kind that will divide opinion, and he himself is – rather modestly – at pains to emphasise that he is no expert on economic policy. But as an economic and social historian, he is more confident in his assessment of how the welfare system grew so dangerously big in the first place. He puts the problem down to three main issues. The first was the complete reorganisation of the welfare system in 1970, which dramatically increased the level of the welfare benefits relative to wages. The second was the introduction in 1979 of the early retirement scheme, which allowed Danes to retire up to five years early. And the third was the loosening of the borders in 1983, which, for the first time in Danish history, saw thousands of immigrants from the Arab world and the Indian subcontinent move to Denmark. Since many of them neither spoke Danish, nor had university degrees, they tragically – and it is nothing short of a national tragedy for Denmark – found it hard to break into what is a highly skilled labour market. As a result, many ended up on benefits. In 2011, only 52% of foreign-born men and 43% of foreign-born women were in work, around 20 percentage points below their Danish-born counterparts. All three of these issues, says Viby, have resulted in an ever-increasing number of people on welfare being paid for by an ever-dwindling number of taxpayers – a fiasco in a system maintained mainly through high taxation. He points at the covers of the two volumes of his book. On the first are some women in a fish factory; on the second are some early-retirees on a golf course. "I can't get it," he says. "These women working in a fish factory are paying taxes to finance the people on the golf courses."

They are also financing a large number of people on unemployment benefits, something which increasingly sticks in the craw of some Danes. Previously, the number of people on benefits was a symbol of pride, at least for those on the left – the sign of a social democracy in good working order. But the media climate has changed, and in certain quarters those in unemployment are today seen less as the responsibility of the state and more as a drain on it. Even though it's Denmark, you come across the same arguments you see in most countries during a downturn – they're benefit-scroungers; they don't deserve it – and you hear exaggerated rumours of youngsters hosting parties to celebrate their admission to benefit schemes.

At the University of Southern Denmark's Centre for Welfare Research, down the road from Sørensen and his robots, Professors Jørn Henrik Petersen and Klaus Petersen explain the numbers. Out of a population of 5.5m, they point out, 1.8m Danes are removed from the labour market – 850,000 on some form of benefits (unemployment; sickness; early retirement; parental leave) and 950,000 more in retirement. But in actual fact, that first group of benefit recipients is not a problem in itself; it is just rendered more significant because the second group, the number of retirees, is likely to grow greatly in size in the coming years.

"The very centre of the problem is obvious if you look to the public sector," says Jørn. "More than half the present labour force working in home-help for the elderly has passed the age of 50. This means that they will retire within the next five to eight years. And that means you have to find their replacements in a declining labour force. And that becomes a hell of a problem."

But where Sørensen sees robots as the answer, the Petersens see young immigrants. In years gone by, many Danes felt that the reason so many so-called "New Danes" remained unemployed was that they were not truly Danish – that they were not culturally wedded to the concept of the collective. It has often even been argued that the Danish welfare state can exist only in a monoculture inhabited by indigenous Danes, and no one else. But really the problem was social, rather than racial. Immigrants found it hard to break into the job market not because they were lazy, but because their skills weren't yet suited to Denmark. They couldn't speak the language, they couldn't get into university, and consequently, in the absence of many manual jobs, couldn't find unemployment. But the Petersens argue that if these "New Danes" were encouraged and trained to work in the social sector, it would kill three birds with one stone. Unemployment among immigrant communities would fall; tax revenues would rise; and there would be enough workers to staff the health service. "A lot of Danes have come to the conclusion that immigrants might from some point of view be a problem," says Jørn. "But equally they might be the answer to another problem. If these immigrants could be integrated into the labour market so that their supply corresponded to the demand, it looks as though they will be part of the solution."

Mainstream debate centres on not just expanding the labour market, but also increasing its productivity, through changes to early retirement, increasing working hours and also reducing the time people can spend on unemployment benefits – it's gone from four years to two, after which you receive a slightly smaller payment. There are now financial incentives for students to finish university earlier and so enter the job market sooner, and moves to tighten the qualification rules for a controversial scheme that allows people to retire long before 60 due to illness.

In general, though, Jørn Henrik Petersen admits the threat to the welfare state is not yet as large as it is in, say, Britain. Cuts to actual services and benefits have been small, and the only major reforms have so far been limited to extending working hours or restricting early retirement. "These are minor problems compared to what's being discussed in other countries. And that is linked to this emphasis on social cohesion, to the belief in a reasonable degree of social equality. Despite all the differences, there is some kind of solidarity in the Danish population. The only group excluded from that? That would be the immigrants."

5. BEING DANISH:
the immigrant's dilemma

"It's like being Danish is something that you're born into."
— Michala Clante Bendixen

About five years ago, as they often did at the time, Danish Broadcasting televised a live debate about Islam. Representing its critics was Mogens Camre, a skinny MEP from the far-right Danish Folkeparti (DFP). On the other side of the table stood Fatih Alev, a liberal imam. Short and stocky, Alev was born and raised in Denmark, and often speaks out against aspects of extremist Islamic culture such as forced marriage.

At some point, the atmosphere turns toxic. Islam, says Mogens Camre, is akin to Nazism. That's an absurd generalisation, replies Alev: Nazism is the kind of rhetoric used by the DFP. Then Camre loses it.

"You have come to this country," he snaps. "Who do

you think you are?"

"I was born in this country," says Alev, calmly. "I'm not an immigrant."

"Stay in your country."

"Denmark is my country. You need to respect your fellow citizens."

"*Du er ikke medborger i mit land*," replies Camre. "You are not a fellow citizen."

It would be nice to be able to say that this conversation (which you can see for yourself in Helle Hansen's excellent documentary *Ordet Fanger*, or "*Words Matter*") was a one-off – analogous with Nick Griffin's one-off appearance on *Question Time*. But it wasn't. Unlike the BNP, the DFP is not a fringe party. It remains the third-largest party in the Danish parliament, and from 2001 until 2011 the centre-right coalition government relied on their support to function. The DFP's politicians were constantly in the news, and – since the government was so reliant on their support – they became powerful policy-makers, pushing through ever more stringent anti-immigration laws.

It was, and to an extent still is, a noxious environment – and its nadir came with the Muhammed cartoons crisis in 2005-6. At the time, rumours swirled of a children's author who wanted to write a book about the prophet Muhammed. The author claimed he couldn't find any illustrators brave enough to draw the prophet – an action Muslims consider offensive – and saw this as a worrying erosion of free speech. The editors at the newspaper *Jyllands-Posten* agreed.

Wanting to show that they wouldn't be dictated to by the customs of another culture, the paper invited 40 established cartoonists to draw Muhammed. Twelve cartoonists complied, and the selection was printed in late September 2005. Some of the selected images were simply portraits of the prophet. One was a piss-take of the whole process – a schoolboy called Mohammed who had written on his blackboard: "*Jyllands-Posten*'s journalists are a bunch of reactionary provocateurs." But two were clearly intended to offend. The first showed Muhammed telling a group of deceased Muslim men that heaven had run out of virgins. The second depicted Muhammed as a terrorist, with a bomb sticking out of his turban.

The cartoons themselves caused considerable offence, but it was what happened next that created a crisis. Despite widespread protests and complaints, *Jyllands-Posten* would not apologise for printing the cartoons. Even more significantly, the then prime minister Anders Fogh Rasmussen refused to meet with a delegation of ambassadors from across the Muslim world who wanted to discuss not just the cartoons, but other recent instances of Islamophobia too. Feeling ignored, a group of Danish Muslims toured the Middle East towards the end of 2005, in an effort to raise awareness about the way Muslims were treated in Denmark. The tour achieved its aim, and at the beginning of 2006, people across the Middle East began to burn the Danish flag, and to boycott Danish goods – costing the Danish economy hundreds of millions of dollars. Several Arab and Asian countries then recalled their ambassadors from Copenhagen, and the crisis became the defining moment of the Danish noughties.

Over the past few years, the issue has been trodden over so many times that the country is tired of discussing it. No firm conclusion was ever reached. Some Danes think the cartoons were a needless provocation. Others think they were an appropriate defence of free speech. Farshad Kholghi is from the latter camp. One of the stars of *The Killing*, Kholghi fled the Iranian revolution for Denmark as a child, and now writes a right-wing column for *Jyllands-Posten* alongside his acting and stand-up work. He justifies the cartoons with an anecdote from one of his stand-up nights. "I was discussing the crisis and defending the cartoonists," says Kholghi, "and the audience were almost offended by my speech. But then this Iranian woman jumped out on stage and told them: "You shut up. I just came from Iran. I was in the streets, and when I said I lived in Denmark, everyone gave me the thumbs up. They said: 'You guys in Denmark, you're so brave, you make fun of the mullahs. That's what we try to do here, but they kill us.' And that was an eye-opener."

But when I meet Fatih Alev, he says this kind of argument misses the point. "We don't have a problem with non-Muslims drawing the prophet Muhammed," says Alev. "They do it. They have done it before. There was a book published around 2002 by a Danish priest called *God is Great*. It's a comparison of Christianity and Islam, and it's been in Danish libraries for many years. But no Muslim has ever objected to it. So the anger in 2005 was not about people drawing the prophet. That's nonsense. The problem was that the cartoonists associated the prophet with terrorism, and that's unacceptable."

This is the heart of the issue: the cartoons weren't really about preserving open debate. They were intended to provoke and humiliate an already marginalised section of society. "Most Muslims value free speech," says Alev. "We appreciate it all the more because of the problems in many of the countries that we come from. But this wasn't about free speech. This was about offending a group in society that already felt very unwelcome. It was a provocation."

To understand where Alev is coming from, you need to see the cartoons in the context of widespread Danish Islamophobia and xenophobia throughout much of the past decade. Put simply, minorities (who form around 10% of the population) – and particularly Muslims (around 3%) – feel got at. In the run-up to the cartoons' publication, minister of culture Brian Mikkelsen had called Islam "medieval". The DFP MP Louise Frevert described Muslims as a tumour that needed to be removed from Europe. Søren Krarup, a DFP MP who doubles as a priest, has described the headscarf as the "equivalent to Communist and Nazi symbols", and thinks that a teacher who wears one is essentially wearing a Nazi uniform. The Koran, he adds, is like Hitler's *Mein Kampf*.

Foreigners were and are still often portrayed in a negative light by the media. "I was used to the verbal attacks and insults being made in the Danish newspapers on a daily basis," says Alev. In 2009, Lars Hedegaard – then a long-standing columnist for the centre-right broadsheet, *Berlingske Tidende* – was arrested for suggesting that Islam allowed men to rape their daughters. In Chapter seven, *The Killing*'s Farshad Kholghi talks about how hard it was to get an Asian part that didn't involve playing a terrorist or a criminal – and that's coming from a man who has himself been criticised for being too critical of Islam. When I visit Denmark, everyone mentions a recent *Politiken* article about an immigrant who impressed at his job. That everyone talks about its publication with such surprise tells its own story.

And then there were the government policies. During the noughties, the centre-right coalition revamped the immigration procedure to include a now notorious points system. In the words of Mads Brandstrup, a political correspondent for *Politiken*, "for any country with brown people, it was basically impossible to get in". The sketch troupe Circusrevy, who broadcast an annual revue on Danish television, wrote a skit that satirised the absurdity of the system. The sketch depicted two would-be Muslim immigrants – Fatima and Ahmed – who wanted to meet the criteria so badly that they bought a bible and traditional Danish clothes, covered their flat in porcelain, started watching porn, and then got divorced. They still didn't pass.

The government also introduced a harsh set of marriage rules – rules sadly not too dissimilar to those announced in

Britain in 2012. In order for a Danish resident to marry someone from outside the EU – or to be reunited with their existing spouse – both parties would have to be older than 24; produce a sizeable deposit; and be earning more than about £30,000 a year. Unless one of them had lived in Denmark for at least 28 years, the couple would have to have been in Denmark, on aggregate, longer than they had lived overseas. The move was justified as a crusade against forced marriages. But in reality, those immigrants who really wanted to get married went to live in Malmø, across the sea in Sweden, and every other immigrant just felt picked on – a feeling that was amplified by later attempts to ban the burqa and the headscarf.

Right-wing MPs argued that the burqa went against Danish values. Muslims argued that you could probably

count the number of Danish burqa-wearers on your hand, and that this was therefore just another attempt to tar a whole minority with the brush of fundamentalism. In fact, more generally, Muslims are frustrated at being lumped into one homogenous group – something this chapter is itself guilty of. Unlike the Muslim community in, say, Germany, which is predominantly Turkish, Danish Muslims come from a very wide range of countries, which in turn sometimes makes solidarity between the different factions difficult.

Through the decade, the buzzword "integration" was constantly used. A Ministry for Integration was established – and you still hear the word all the time. Its meaning changes depending on the context. Sometimes people ask: how can we better integrate different groups of immigrants and Danes? But then there's a more frustrated question: why won't foreigners integrate? The first example sounds vaguely inclusive, but the second is slightly oppressive. Literally, the word implies some kind of mutual effort on the part of both Danes and newcomers. But often it is simply used to mean one-way assimilation.

The role the DFP played in the creation of these ideas and policies showed how far to the right the Danish immigration debate had shifted. Back in the 80s, the likes of Søren Krarup were ridiculed by those from the centre-right. After Krarup ran a large newspaper advert asking Danes to stop giving money to refugees – "No, not a single krone" – the prime minister, Venstre's Poul Hartling, called him fanatical and hysterical. Other Venstre politicians responded by personally collecting money on the streets. When the DFP was founded a decade later – following a split from the far-right Progress Party in 1995 – it was ridiculed by those from the left and the centre-right alike. The Conservative leader Hans Engell said he doubted the DFP would ever form the basis of a coalition government. In 1999, the Social Democrat prime minister Poul Nyrup Rasmussen told DFP politicians that "no matter how hard you try, you will never be decent."

But times change. In the 2001 election, the DFP won 12% of the vote, becoming Denmark's third-largest parliamentary party – a position they've held ever since. As a result, they entered into a loose alliance with the same centre-right parties – Venstre and the Conservatives – that had tried to distance themselves from the DFP during the previous decade. And as the documentary *Ordet Fanger* shows, Venstre's new prime minister Anders Fogh Rasmussen started mimicking – to a word – the reactionary language Pia Kjaersgaard (the one-time DFP leader) had been using ten years earlier. "Denmark can't be the benefits office for the whole world," said Kjaersgaard in 1993. "Denmark can't be the benefits office for the whole world," said Fogh Rasmussen in 2003.

Since the Social Democrats were re-elected in 2011, the spotlight has shifted – slightly. The DFP aren't in the news every week, and Danish debate is preoccupied with the financial crisis.

Meanwhile, the government has thrown immigrants a few olive branches. Immigrants who want to marry a foreigner now have to have lived in Denmark for only 26 years, rather than 28. In a symbolic move, the Ministry of Integration has folded and been incorporated into other departments. The notorious points system has been repealed – though, like the closure of the integration ministry, this change is largely cosmetic. Points or not, Denmark's immigration rules are still almost as strict as they were before. In fact, though they've hit the pause button on the xenophobic rhetoric, the Social Democrats haven't exactly rewound everything either. Nyrup Rasmussen may have once called the DFP "indecent" – but a decade on, his Social Democrat successors aren't doing a great deal to revoke their policies. "It's not so easy for them though," argues Alev. "Even among the supporters of the Social Democrats there are a lot of people who could potentially shift to the Dansk Folkeparti."

Outside of politics, xenophobia still regularly rears its head in Danish public life. In April 2012, a regional newspaper reported that "*Neger stjal bil fra 80-arig*" – or "Negro stole car from 80-year-old." It was a conscious choice, the editor argued. "I do not think it is an offensive word," he said. "If he had been a red-head, I would have written that. If he had been bald, I would have written that."

A month later, it emerged that the Danish Film Institute had rejected a producer's funding application because, among other reasons, "Films featuring cast members with another ethnic background haven't shown to be especially sellable in the provinces."

•

From the outside, Fatih Alev's mosque doesn't really look like a place of worship. On a housing estate in Nørrebro, and three floors up a tower-block caked in graffiti, the Danish Islamic Centre is actually a four-bedroom flat that has been hastily converted into a makeshift prayer centre. When I sit in on Friday prayers one week, it's easy to see why many Muslims feel so isolated. Their places of worship are all a bit like this. Unlike the Danish Church, which receives public funding through tax revenues, minority religions get no help from the state – and as a result there is only one purpose-built mosque in Denmark. And the sense of isolation that this causes is exacerbated by the reluctance of politicians to visit those temporary sites that do exist.

"In many other European countries, government officials don't have a problem with visiting a mosque in times of crisis or during an important religious festival," says Alev. "This is very important – it helps the Muslim society to feel at home and included, to see that they are being officially recognised in the society. But you don't see this in Denmark. You don't see it because the government representatives don't want to be seen in the company of someone who may be, later on, portrayed as an extremist, as a radical person who said this and that and so forth."

At Friday prayers, I meet a 22-year-old man called Wasim. He is keen to talk about what it feels like to be a young Muslim in Denmark, so we later have a coffee at Copenhagen University, where he studies sociology. As soon as we sit down, Wasim cuts to the chase.

"I was born here," he says, "but I don't feel like a Dane."

Why not? I ask.

"Look at the political system," he replies – and he's off. "For the last ten years, they have been against us. Every time. We are only seven to ten per cent of the population, and yet every time you look at the news it's about us. Of course, there are a few who make trouble, but they are a small part. Look at this university. There are so many Asian students. But they never talk about us. I don't think I've really read about a foreigner, like me, who's doing well in education. A few days ago I read about a foreigner who was doing well in business, and the time before that was a long time ago. Why is it like that? We have so many successful stories. But we only read about the bad sides of the foreigners."

Wasim is against forced marriage and the burqa, but he felt stigmatised by the laws that tried to ban them. He felt they were just a smokescreen for making immigrants feel even more unwelcome. The final straw came at 18 – when, having lived in Denmark all his life, he had to apply for permanent residency, a stepping stone towards full citizenship.

"I was born here but because my parents were not Danish, I couldn't get citizenship by birth," he explains. "So when I was 18, I had to prove that I was Danish – even though I was born in Denmark, lived here all my life and got my education in Denmark, just like any other Dane." He raises his voice. "And when I applied, I had to wait six fucking months – sorry for my language – even though I was born here. The son of an EU citizen would only have to wait one month. Are we not the same? Things like this made me realise that it's not my country any more."

He calms down. "Sorry to get angry, but I hate this law. It's like I'm from another world. It's like I'm not even human. That's why I don't feel like a Dane. Struggle is a big word, but I had an identity struggle. I gave up about half a year ago. I just realised that I'm a Pakistani in this country. I'm a foreigner."

Wasim speaks wistfully about his cousins in the UK, who he says don't have this problem. "They call themselves British Muslims. And they're the same age as me, and born in Britain. How can that difference happen?" He makes it clear that he's not angry at ordinary Danes, just the people at the top. "I love the Danes," he says, "and I love Denmark. There is a good welfare state. If you're out of work, you get benefits. There's free education, free medical care. But for me, I don't feel accepted by the politicians. I want acceptance of my identity."

Wasim claims that his complaint is common among many other cosmopolitan "New Danes", or Danes of foreign origin. "There are many, many foreigners who tell me: 'Wasim, this is not my country.' They're well-educated, from Danish universities, and they're saying, 'Well, okay, if they don't accept me, I have a Master's, I can get a job somewhere else.'"

Wasim constantly mentions how many Muslims he knows at university, and how employable they are. This is refreshing, because a stereotypically bigoted criticism of immigrants in Denmark is that they are uneducated and work-shy. It's true – the stats aren't great. As noted in the previous chapter, only 52% of foreign-born men and 43% of foreign-born women were in work in 2011, around 20 percentage points below their Danish-born counterparts. Before the financial crisis, immigrants' net contribution to the welfare state had almost reached parity, but this has since dropped again. As a result, there is a perception that Denmark and its glorious welfare state can only work as a monoculture unsoiled by outsiders.

This isn't particularly fair, says Michala Clante Bendixen, a campaigner for immigrant rights and a board member of the charity Refugees Underground. "We consider the welfare system to be perfect, and that if anyone wants to join it, it's their problem to get into it," argues Bendixen. "They have to find their own way, and if they don't succeed, it's their fault. They're not doing it well enough. They're lazy. But we're not looking at integration as a two-way system where we also have to open up to get new people into the system. We just say 'they should do more to integrate'. If you don't speak the language perfectly, if you don't have the connections, the experience, the education – you're left out.

"Danish society has actually done very little to try to find out what the problem is. Why is it difficult for immigrants to enter the labour market? How can we help them to enter the labour market? Can we give them the resources to work, instead of hitting them on the head and saying, 'You don't want to work'? Can we prepare the work market better? Maybe it's not absolutely necessary to speak fluent Danish in order to have certain positions within a company."

Part of the problem is that some immigrants don't have the grades to get into university, and so can't find employment within Denmark's highly skilled jobs market. One answer is to change the way applicants are assessed – so that they're judged on potential, rather than just exam results. Another left-field option comes from Nille Juul-Sørensen, head of the Danish Design Institute, who wants the government to help young New Danes to set up businesses. "Many are top-notch students, but many are not the guys who go through academia," he argues. "But they're really good at trading. You want good vegetables, go to Nørrebro. This is actually a golden pot for entrepreneurs. So why don't we take their kids and say: 'We believe in you, we believe you can do the start-ups, it's in your culture.' If they don't want to do maths, can we help them set up a company selling music?"

Alev is hopeful that things will change. "There's a development, a process going on. Look at the professions young people [of foreign ancestry] are taking. They're not just studying medicine or engineering – they are more and more confident. They're studying archaeology, anthropology. People say that immigration has destroyed the fundaments of our welfare society, but these immigrants are going to boost up the Danish economy and we'll be better funded than ever. It'll be very entertaining to read all of these [xenophobic] statements 20 years from now."

In Denmark, the average women's wage is much lower than the men's one, but it is still a great source of Danish pride that there are almost as many women in work as men. However, as we have seen, the percentage of foreign-born women in work (43) is much lower than the overall figure for women (70) – which leads some Danes to conclude that immigrant communities are misogynist and therefore unsuited to participating in the welfare state, which relies on as many people paying tax as possible.

"We expect foreign women who come here to work – and I think that's a good idea," says Bendixen. "But you can't expect them to do it [immediately] because it's not natural for them like it's natural for us… If you asked the women, they would very much like to work. That's what we hear all the time. They would *love* to have a job, and they envy the Danish women for being able to make their own money. So it's not because they don't want to – it's because they don't have the resources or the background to do it. So we should try to educate these women and cooperate with the work market to create jobs for these women without an education."

Alev thinks that some immigrants do have simplistic views when it comes to the role of women of society. But he argues that this is a social problem, not a racial or religious one – and that it's become less of an issue over time. Yes, he says: some immigrants who come from remote rural areas of the Arab and Asian world are stuck in a time warp. But after they've been in Denmark for a while, they start to change their tune.

"The integration debate in Denmark has been very much based on religious and ethnic differences," agrees Clante Bendixen. "But every time you look at a research report, you find that these are social problems, not ethnic ones. Young boys starting fires aren't doing that because it's in their ethnic tradition. It's because they're poor and unemployed and stacked together in areas where only foreigners and poor people live."

•

In City Hall Square, in the middle of Copenhagen, 500 protesters are holding a rally. They're a more diverse bunch than most crowds in Denmark. Some are black, some Kurdish, others Arab, and the rest are white Danes. Hoisted above their heads is a banner that reads: "We want to live." These are refugees – or at least most of them are – and they are protesting at their treatment by the Danish authorities, and at the way they are often perceived as either benefit-scroungers or criminals. There are around 4500 refugees in Denmark, and while their case is being considered, nearly all of them must live in camps far removed from mainstream

Danish life. To illustrate their isolation, the protesters have today marched from a camp 16 kilometres outside Copenhagen.

Zach is one of the refugees. He came to Denmark from Kenya last August, fearing for his life for reasons he does not want me to print. He is still waiting to find out if he can stay – and in the meantime he has had plenty of time to contemplate the problems with the Danish asylum system.

The camps are the most obvious problem, he says. The rooms are cramped – many stuffed with up to four people – and researchers from the University of Copenhagen think they spark mental problems in children. They're also very isolated. At Zach's camp in rural Auderod, the refugees live five kilometres from the nearest station, which is itself one and a half hours from the nearest city, Copenhagen. The ticket costs 108 kroner – unaffordable for refugees, who receive only 50 kroner a day (around £6) in pocket money. Zach would gladly work to earn more money – but, like all refugees, he's not allowed. And as he's over 23, he doesn't even get free Danish lessons. "You're in a country where you don't speak the language," says Zach, "and you don't have the opportunity to learn it." To get any kind of Danish tuition, he must make a journey he can't afford, to a charity-cum-safespace for refugees in Copenhagen called Trampoline House.

Not everyone has this experience. At a refugee centre in Holbaek, Mohammed – an Afghan who was granted asylum very quickly – is full of praise for the system. In Ringkøbing, in west Jutland, I meet a Bosnian Muslim called Damir Zvirkic who fled a massacre in 1993 and was part of a group apparently granted asylum after a personal intervention from Margrethe, the Danish queen. Zvirkic feels Danish now, even when he goes back to Bosnia on holiday. "I miss my old country," he says. "But when we're at the end of our holiday, and I say to my children: 'we have to go home' – I'm talking about Denmark. And when you start to call Denmark your home, that's a sign."

But for Zach, the asylum process remains one of trauma. "There is always a fear that tomorrow they will send you a letter saying that you will be deported to the same country you have left. You never know when that is happening. At the end of the process, whether or not you get asylum, your life has changed. You've been living in the camp for one, two, three, four, five years. Every night you are woken up by people screaming. You are surrounded by people who often cannot communicate with you. You can't go to school. You can't work. Your life is very limited."

Denmark is not alone. Many countries – not least Britain – haven't properly worked out how to come to terms with immigration. And unlike much of western Europe, Denmark doesn't have much of a colonial past, and so has had less time than most to come to terms with the concept of multi-culturalism. But the country definitely has a problem. "It's like being Danish is something that you're born into," says Bendixen. "So what can you do if you come as a foreigner? How can you solve that? If you don't look like a Dane, and your name is not a traditional Danish one, then it's not enough, even if you were born here. You'll never become a real Dane."

But does that make Denmark xenophobic? Or even racist? It's more complex than that, argues Fatih Alev. To understand why some Danes behave as they do, we need to look at Denmark in its historical context. "Somebody needs to say it: Denmark is a country with minority complexes because it's a small country. Previously, it was a bigger country, ruling over Sweden and Norway. But now it is reduced to only this country. So I wouldn't just use the word 'racism', it's not as simple as that. There are historical, cultural reasons why the Danes need to see themselves as a homogenous people."

Richard Jenkins, an anthropologist whose career has centred on the study of Danishness, explores these reasons in considerable detail in his brilliant book, *Being Danish*. The very loose gist of one of his arguments is that the Danes' intolerance of outsiders is ironically rooted in the values of cohesion and tolerance preached by Nicolai Grundtvig in the 19th century. "The solution that was found to the problems of Denmark in the mid-19th century," writes Jenkins, "has created a new problem in the present."

This might seem strange, given that Grundtvig's ideas promoted democracy and social engagement, and are theoretically therefore transferable to a modern context. But it's important to remember how these progressive ideas rose to such prominence in the first place. In 1864, Denmark had just lost the last bits of its Baltic empire, and the population that remained felt humiliated. Once a multinational commonwealth, Denmark was now a tiny monoculture. Danes suddenly found that they were a people without an identity – and used Grundtvig's ideas to create one. And so these ideas – enlightened as they may have been – became a means of defining and justifying Denmark's newfound homogeneity. In this way, Danes became exclusive through their inclusivity, intolerant through their tolerance – which helps to explain some of the contradictions in today's society. Take, says Jenkins, "the warmth and relaxation of *hygge* on a cold winter's evening. *Hygge*, however, is double-edged: it is necessarily exclusionary, because there are always boundaries to a magic circle, and it may also be controlling, particularly when it verges on the compulsory. Intolerance, actual or potential, is never too far away. The most obvious manifestations of this other face of Danish homogeneity are the Jante Law – small-minded, corrosive envy of achievement and difference – and xenophobia and racism, the total rejection of difference."

The exclusivity is often unconscious. Look at the ubiquity of Dannebrog, the Danish flag. At a birthday party I attend in Copenhagen, the flat is festooned with versions of it. When I go to dinner with a family in Odense, they greet me at the door waving it. Sure, my hosts were hamming things up for their English visitor – but what they were doing was not unusual. Whenever something remotely festive happens in Denmark, the Danes crack out their flag.

But as Jenkins explains in great detail in *Being Danish*, this flag-waving often isn't consciously nationalistic. Certainly, the DFP have an elaborate flag-waving ceremony at their party conferences. But for most people, it's just what you do when you hold a party, or when infrequent visitors call. People thought it was strange when I suggested it was nationalistic. And this is telling, because it shows that nationalism is so engrained in Danish culture that people sometimes don't even notice that it's there.

It's the same with Christianity. Danes aren't particularly religious. At a confirmation service I'm invited to just north of Copenhagen, it's clear that the congregation doesn't come here very often. They have no idea what they're doing. The service is one long Mexican wave – a ripple of parents continuously standing up and sitting down because they're copying the people in front, who have as little clue as they do.

But what's significant is that these families – even though many of them don't believe in God – have turned up in such large numbers. There are many more people here than you'd expect at a British confirmation service, and the parties afterwards will be more numerous and more extravagant than anything a British 14-year-old could expect after tasting bread and wine for the first time. What this suggests is that though Danes may not be fervent Christians, the Danish Church and its traditions still have an important role in Danish culture, and in the way that children come of age as Danes. Even at "non-firmation" parties – confirmation for those who don't want to go to church – you could argue that Danish Lutheranism looms large through its absence.

Danes, then, may not be fervent believers. Even Grundtvig, a priest, said he was a citizen first and a Christian second. But the attainment of Danishness still to an extent involves buying into the trappings of the Danish Church – both culturally and financially: 80% of Danes pay 1% of their earnings to the Church. In turn, this perhaps shows why some Danes are culturally so wary of foreign religions – and why newcomers, particularly Muslims, might find it hard to attain Danishness, since it is founded in experiences they clearly cannot achieve.

6. WONDERFUL, WONDERFUL COPENHAGEN

"Copenhageners cycle to live, but they don't live to cycle"
– Mikael Colvile-Andersen

One November day in 2006, a journalist called Mikael Colvile-Andersen was cycling to his office at Danish Broadcasting. At some point, he got out his camera and took a picture. "It was this woman on a bike, very elegantly dressed," remembers Colvile-Andersen. "The lights had turned green but she hadn't moved yet. There are ladies cycling past on the right, guys roaring past on the left. But she hadn't moved yet. And I just thought, oh, that's nice. Click. It wasn't the girl. It wasn't the bike. It was my morning commute."

Colvile-Andersen put the photo up on his Flickr page, where he has a large following, and thought no more about it. "But then the comments started coming in. 'Hey, dude!

How does she ride a bike in a skirt? And boots?!' And I was like: what the fuck are these guys talking about? It was a completely alien concept to me, these questions."

Cycling is normal in Copenhagen. In *Borgen*, the prime minister cycles to work – and it's not particularly hard to imagine Helle Thorning-Schmidt doing the same in real life. When I visit parliament, the forecourt outside is stuffed with as many bikes as the quad of an Oxbridge college. Elsewhere in the city, at least a third of Copenhageners cycle to work or school – and they don't wear lycra. They don't need to. The city is built for cycling. It's flat, for a start – but it also has the infrastructure. In greater Copenhagen, there are 1000 kilometres of bike lanes – and you get them all over Denmark. Last Christmas Eve, Colvile-Andersen cycled – laden with presents – all the way to Roskilde, 30 kilometres to the west of Copenhagen, and never left a bike lane. There's one on every busy street – sometimes two lanes deep, and always protected from the road by a kerb.

Cyclists have their own traffic lights, which let them set off a few seconds before the cars. On some new routes, if you cycle at a steady 20 kilometres per hour, the lights will automatically stay green for miles. And as you cruise through the city, you'll see a staggering number of bike shops. On several streets, every fourth shop is a "cykel vaerksted". Each sells bikes that are made for the city – bikes with a kick-stand and a mechanism that locks the bike to itself so that you don't waste time searching for a lamppost to padlock your wheels to. Many Copenhagen families don't own a car – but one in five has a cargo bike that fits two or three kids. Few cyclists jump the lights – the system works so well that they don't need to.

All of this helps explain why a woman cycling to work one day in 2006 wouldn't think twice about wearing a skirt and boots. In Copenhagen, that's what you do. You don't ride a mountain bike, and you don't wear lycra. There is a campaign to make helmets compulsory, but you most likely won't wear one either. You dress as you would normally, and, this being Copenhagen, you look pretty stylish. "Do I wear special clothes when I get on the bus?" asks Colvile-Andersen. "No. We dress for our destination, not our journey."

But judging from the reception he received on Flickr, Colvile-Andersen quickly realised that this wasn't the case in most other places. "I became curious," he says. "I thought, wow, the whole world thinks it's pretty wild here. So I started taking more pictures of these elegantly dressed Copenhageners on their bikes that month, and continued to put them up on Flickr. Then in 2007, I started a blog." That blog was called Copenhagen Cycle Chic, and it soon developed a cult following. "It just poured in. A hundred people a day on the blog, within two weeks. I was like: woah. What's up with that stuff? I don't understand it. I'll just take more photos. And that's when it really took off."

Nearly six years on, the blog and its social media pages get over 20,000 hits every day. It has spawned around 200 copy-cat sites worldwide, a spin-off book, and, in

Copenhagen, a team of contributing photographers who include the former Danish ambassador to Afghanistan. Most Danes are still a bit non-plussed – "A guy with a blog about bikes," explains Colvile-Andersen, "is like a guy in Greenland with a blog about snow" – but he says that some Copenhageners now actively try to get photographed. "I've heard there's a game. 'Oh, I put my best dress on today and cycled down the streets they usually photograph for Cycle Chic. And, damn! I didn't get snapped.'"

For Colvile-Andersen, the blog has sparked a career swerve. "After the blog started running, people would email me saying: 'I'm from the department of transport in, I dunno, Shitsville, Arkansas. What is that blue paint in the cycling lane in your picture? Literally, what is it made of?"

Around a third of Copenhageners cycle to work

Through answering these questions, Colvile-Andersen developed a greater understanding of how urban planning works – and then realised he could do a better job of it than most. He now runs a cycling consultancy – Copenhagenize – that advises politicians around the world about how to make their cycling infrastructure more like Copenhagen's. And wherever he goes, a Cycle Chic fan is always on hand to lend him a bike.

He thinks that part of the problem in other countries is that cycling is promoted using eco-arguments, or through the creation of a geeky cycling subculture. "The bicycle advocates, the avid cyclists," he says, "they're a sub-culture. And the nature of subcultures is that you want other people to share your hobby. Whether you're a bowler or a synchro-nised swimmer, you've got to understand my love of it, and you've got to copy it. If you don't, then you're not really a cyclist. You can't just ride the old Raleigh that you found in your grandmother's old house in Bournemouth. You've got to have the right bike – otherwise it's not real." Copenhageners, on the other hand, just use bikes to get around town. According to government surveys, half of them say they cycle simply because it's fast. Only a third cycle because it's healthy. They cycle to live, but they don't live to cycle.

Not so long ago, though, most of them didn't do either. In the economic boom following the Second World War, everyone bought cars, and there were plans to eliminate cycling as a mode of transport, and to make the roads as suitable as possible for motoring. The last tram in Copenhagen went out of service in 1972, and only one in ten commuters went by bike. There's a famous picture from 1980 of Nyhavn, the pastel-coloured wharf in central Copenhagen that is now one of the most popular spots in the city. Today, it is pedestrianised and lined with cafés and boats. In 1980, it was essentially one big car park.

"Why not?" says a man called Jan Gehl, dripping with sarcasm. "It's the perfect parking space. The cars have a great view from there."

Gehl is the godfather of Copenhagen's open-plan streets, and perhaps the patron saint of cyclists worldwide. Throughout 1962, Gehl – then a young architecture student – spent one day every week sitting on a street called Strøget. It's pronounced a bit like "stroll" – fittingly so, because it was the first pedestrianised high street in Europe. At 3.2 kilometres long, it remains the longest. Gehl was concerned at the way Copenhagen's Modernist urban planners were eating away at cycling lanes, and at public space. He was convinced that public spaces that encouraged interaction were the secret to both a happy city and the Danish concept of cooperation – but he needed some data to back him up. At the time, there was none.

"Nothing was known," Gehl says in this magical voice that has the same reassuring effect on cyclists that Dumbledore has on Hogwarts. "People had never been the subject of study in cities, ever. It was taken for granted that people moved about in public spaces. It was only when the traffic started to pressurise life, and when the Modernist planners started to discourage the use of space between buildings that we realised there was a need for research."

And that was why Gehl, notepad in hand, could be found every week in 1962, strolling up and down Strøget. "This was some of the pioneering stuff," Gehl says, proudly tapping *Life Between Buildings*, one of the many books that came out of the research. "Sitting there, watching people. Finding out: what is a day like? What is a week like? What is a year like? What is the difference between summer, autumn, winter? What happens when there is a festival? A fire? The queen's birthday? We had to collect all the basics about human behaviour in public spaces. How you kiss and how you walk, dance – whatever you do in cities, where you do it, how you do it."

Over time, Gehl's research – which soon spread to other cities – became more and more influential. "We have been able to show that the more square metres you pedestrianise, the more people will use the city. It's good for democracy and good for inclusion that we mingle in the public space. It's good for your health, and good for the environment."

In Copenhagen, more and more cycle lanes were reintroduced, and pedestrianisation spread to the streets around Strøget – to the extent that today, Copenhagen's centre is one of the most relaxing city centres I've been to. It makes you wish that someone would do something similar to the cesspit around Leicester Square.

Across one whole wall in Gehl's office is a vast streetmap

of San Francisco, one of the cities he is currently advising. Along one long strip of road, he has drawn a box and labelled it "living room". It sums up his ideology, and, in fact, the ethos of Copenhagen: the city as one big sofa.

But the transition wasn't all down to Gehl. "I have done nothing in the city," he says, very modestly. "There's a widespread rumour that the pedestrianisation is because of me. No. I used the pedestrianisation as a laboratory for my studies. But then we can see a very interesting dialogue between university and town hall. Our studies encouraged them enormously to do more projects. The mayor even wrote to me to say: 'If you hadn't done those studies, we politicians would not have dared to make Copenhagen what it is today.'" Gehl's eyes twinkle. "I like that."

Gehl admits the mentality is born as much from necessity as idealism. On a white sheet of paper, he draws me a timeline which is now stuck up on my wall at home, and on it he underlines the year 1973 several times. "The oil crisis," he says, referring to the year that the petrol producers in the Arab world stopped exporting oil in protest at the West's support of Israel during the Yom Kippur War. Denmark was particularly badly hit, and even though they later found oil in the North Sea, it made Danes fearful of ever being so reliant on fossil fuel and, by extension, cars. It helps explain why Denmark now makes just under half the world's wind turbines, and why Copenhagen turned, once again, to cycling.

"We started to have car-free days. Not because of a love

of mankind, but because of a lack of petroleum. Everybody rejoiced because it was wonderful having car-free Sundays. And they realised it would be clever to go back to bicycles."

The mentality stuck. By 2025 it aims to be the world's first carbon-neutral capital. Along with a third of his fellow Copenhageners, Jan Gehl – 76 years young – still cycles to work. And year after year, Copenhagen is named as one of the world's most livable cities.

There's a reason for that – lots of them, in fact. Copenhagen's big enough to house several distinct districts (Indre By, the shopping district in the middle; suburban Amager to the east; hip Vesterbro in the south-west, nestling below multicultural Nørrebro; and then Østerbro, Denmark's answer to Notting Hill) but small enough to cross it in 20 minutes – on a bike, naturally. The streets are wide and lined with graceful rococo houses and there's rarely a crap building in site. There's a beach within striking distance, a huge outdoor swimming pool in the middle of the harbour, or if you just want to sit, rather than take a dip, you can pop along to Christiania, the 40-year-old anarchist commune that jostles against the lake in Christianshavn.

Culturally, the city is buzzing. As explored in Chapter two, Copenhagen is where the world's foodies currently go to eat. Its television studios are the home of Danish noir. In Bjarke Ingels, it has spawned the starchitect of the moment. In Distortion – essentially a mobile rave that tours the city's districts each year in June – it has one of northern Europe's most unusual music festivals. Vesterbro is a sort of Shoreditch-lite, with new bars and galleries sprouting all the time. Copenhagen has the second-biggest homes in Europe – and they're are almost all heated and cooled from a central hub (rather than on an individual basis), which has resulted in a 70% reduction in carbon emissions.

Twenty-five years ago, this would have been hard to imagine. "Copenhagen was nearly bankrupt," remembers the city's head of planning, Anne Skovbro, whose offices are in the same city hall that features prominently in the first series of *The Killing*. (Skovbro's claim to fame: her leg features in one of the shots.) "We were an old industrial harbour city that had lost most of its industry to Jutland and China."

Unemployment was high, infrastructure was failing, the housing system was in crisis, and welfare costs had spiralled. Urban renewal was urgently needed – and there was a consensus at government level that if it was to be done at all, it needed to be done properly. So the state bailed out the city – and it was then, in the late 80s and early 90s, that Copenhagen really got going.

"We had to ensure this change from an old industrial city, with a lot of brown-field sites," says Skovbro, "to an efficient, knowledge-based city with new housing development and a sustainable infrastructure."

The beginnings of a subway system were set in motion. New neighbourhoods to the north and south of the city were planned – and they're now reaching completion.

Further investment was put into cycling lanes, and more green spaces were created. Flats were knocked together to create bigger living spaces, and three new architectural jewels were built at strategic intervals along the waterfront – a new opera house, a national library and a theatre. And to pay for all this, the city sold off large tracts of land to the south of the city at Ørestad, in a Faustian pact that has seen the emergence of a very un-Danish, neo-Ballardian development on the city's southern fringes. But more on that later.

The urban revival came hand in hand with a cultural one. Most obviously, there were the Dogme film-makers – Lars von Trier and Thomas Winterberg are the most successful – and then there were the art dealers. Copenhagen's National Gallery and Humlebaek's Louisiana Gallery had long housed impressive collections, but there were very few commercial galleries. In the late 80s, Mikael Andersen was one of the first Copenhageners to establish one.

"It was difficult. Copenhagen was very provincial 25 years ago," he remembers. "We didn't have a gallery system. At the time, artists would show their work at an institution every year, as a group. We live in a very social democratic society, and people were suspicious of commercial art. They thought commercial galleries were just trying to get money out of artists."

And when he opened his space in Bredgade, only a mile from Strøget, people scoffed at him for straying so far – as they saw it – from the centre. But Andersen had the last laugh. There are now ten galleries within 100 metres of his, and at the private view I attend, there are collectors from all over the world. These days, though, the trendiest galleries are on the other side of town, not far from the former red-light district in Vesterbro. What's happened here mirrors what's happened in Copenhagen over the past two decades: Vesterbro has been transformed from a gritty, working-class neighbourhood into the place where all the cool crowd hang out. The centre of this transition has been the old meatpacking district, which still functions as such today, but now also houses an array of bars, galleries, cafes and clubs. If you turn up there at four in the morning, you'll see clubbers tottering home to sleep, and butchers rolling up their shutters to start the working day. It's a meat market in more ways than one.

I'm A Kombo, the pop-up chefs in Chapter two, have their kitchen there. A few metres away, there's the Karriere bar, founded by the artist Jeppe Hein – whose work was shown at the Hayward Gallery in 2012 – and his sister Laerke. Once one of the hottest joints in town, it's crammed with furniture designed by Hein's artist friends – Carsten Holler, Dan Graham and Olafur Eliasson among them. Hein built the bar itself, which drifts very slowly sideways as the night goes on. If you don't keep an eye out, your drink will end up half a metre north of where you left it.

Coming to a place like Karriere, you realise how Copenhagen could have become so hip, so quick: everyone knows each other, and many of them share a camaraderie that helps speed up change. Next door to the bar is the V1 Gallery, run by the Heins' friend Jesper Elg. Tonight, Elg's holding a party for a new show. If he's in town, the architect Bjarke Ingels will probably be there. As the night wears on, Trentemøller, the DJ whose work can be heard in the latest Almodóvar film, will spin a few tracks. When Trentemøller goes on tour, he'll be joined on the drums by the fashion

A mural by Kissmama in Vesterbro

designer Henrik Vibskov, who – wait for it – knows Elg from their art school days in London in the late 90s. To round off the set, there's Thomas Fleurquin, busily finalising preparations for this year's Distortion festival, a week that'll see 130,000 ravers engage in activities that – in a blog titled "Distortion and the Decline of Civilisation" – the right-wing broadsheet *Jyllands-Posten* will later label: "infernal noise, senseless drinking, vomit, piss, fornication, and – above all – destruction."

It's an article that neatly encapsulates Denmark's contradictions. Denmark is at once a deeply conservative place and a very tolerant one. It spawned the Muhammed cartoons in 2006 – and yet in 1989 it was the first country to legalise same-sex partnerships. It's a dichotomy further illustrated by two demonstrations that snaked past city hall on consecutive weeks in May. The first highlighted Denmark's darker side – a protest at Denmark's harsh treatment of asylum seekers. The second was a march in celebration of marijuana that followed a float of dreadlocked reggae singers all the way to Christiania, the military base turned semi-autonomous anarchist commune. Home to 850 Christianites, as well as several bars, shops and meditation rooms, Christiania has long housed an open drugs trade to which the authorities turn a blind eye. It's a place of great symbolic importance to the hippies of Europe. If the government ever did seriously try to smash it, one local claims, every stoner on the continent would come to defend it.

As the march dissipates outside the gates of Christiania, I take a look around. Lots of Copenhageners come here to relax by the lake, or find cheap food – but before long I find the thing that the place is most famous for: the Green Light District, a market filled with stalls that sell rocks of hash for a tenner. A shirtless man lies vomiting on the floor, and as I follow the puke I see its cause – a wheelbarrow full of weed that teenagers are gulping down with the help of a fat glass bong. Dizzy and bloodshot, they then slope to the floor – but only the topless chap is particularly worse for wear. At some point, someone somewhere calls for an ambulance, and after a few minutes the paramedics arrive. Mainstream Denmark has a strained relationship with the Christianites (a reporter who recently tried to film a drug deal was stripped naked and unceremoniously ejected) and so they won't enter the Green Light District unless it's absolutely necessary. As a result, there's an awkward few moments while the medics linger on its perimeter, tentatively gauging whether their presence is really needed. It's fraught – but it also somehow feels very cooperative, very Danish. The foot soldiers of the welfare state on the one side, the hippies on the other – and both of them trying to resolve the stand off through silent diplomacy.

This delicate relationship between state and counter-culture hasn't always been so carefully managed. In 2011, the site was temporarily closed to visitors after a disagree-ment between the Christianites and the government about its future. In December 2006, the biggest riots in Danish his-tory broke out in Nørrebro after the authorities announced plans to evict another non-hierarchical community: the Ungdomshuset (or 'Youth House'). Thousands of protest-ers set up burning barricades and threw fireworks at the police, who shot back – to much outrage – with tear gas.

Nearly 300 rioters were arrested, but it wasn't until the following March that the Youth House was finally evicted. Special Forces stormed the building with a military helicopter, and then coated it in foam to protect it from Molotov cocktails. It didn't help. The barricades returned, rioting resumed, a school was ransacked and 690 people were arrested inside three days in what *Le Monde Diplomatique* called "a laboratory experience in police repression".

Copenhagen's smallness is the secret to its creativity. But on the flipside, it has also forced Danes to look overseas for their inspiration. "Because this is a small country, we are focussed on what's going on outside," says Vibskov, sitting in his studio, hunched over a dust-coated MacBook Pro as interns rush to and fro carrying blocks of wood. They're putting the finishing touches to an art installation that will shortly be transported to Mallorca. "If something is popular outside Denmark, music-wise, people accept it *inside* Denmark. And it's such a small society that if one thing gets accepted, everyone does it." It's an attitude that can be constraining, he says. "If something is wild or crazy, it has to be accepted by others before it is accepted here. Some of the stuff I do is not particularly Scandinavian, maybe a little strange. But if I show it in Paris, people here go: 'Ohhh, I see. It's really good.' The Raveonettes were a Danish band living in New York. And when they got picked up by *Rolling Stone* magazine as the best new band, suddenly everyone here went: 'Oh yeah! Cool.'"

But Elg thinks this international outlook has also had a

positive effect: it's given his generation wider horizons, and in doing so has made them much more ambitious than their forebears. They've thrown off the constraints of the Jante Law – a traditional Danish mindset that is critical of anyone who has ideas above their station – and instead they've tried to compete with what's going on elsewhere in Europe. "It's this experience of seeing things happening in other parts of the world and realising: 'Okay, we can actually do this in Copenhagen.' There's this wish to change Copenhagen and make it more interesting for those of us who live here."

Danish self-confidence is improving, says Søren Sveistrup, the man who created *The Killing*. "Now, young people think they can conquer the world. It wasn't like that 20 years ago."

No one represents this newfound swagger better than the architect Bjarke Ingels. In the space of just six years, the 38-year-old and his firm BIG (pronounced like the adjective) have become the most talked about young architects in the world. In New York, he's building a pyramid-shaped skyscraper, while in Copenhagen he tried (unsuccessfully) to plonk a large ski-slope on top of a power station. He's building a new museum in Mexico, a national library in Kazakhstan, a new city hall for the capital of Estonia, and at some point, Ingels has found the time to draw a comic book about his architectural ideals.

He does all this with a brash confidence that can wind people up the wrong way. "He's rude, he's loud, and he builds skyscrapers," one prominent London-based architecture critic tells me. "He's breaking all the rules. It's a case of killing the father."

Traditionally, the fathers of Danish architecture were obsessed by the context of their work – the role buildings play in their surroundings. They all read Jan Gehl at architecture school, and so they were brought up to make their buildings blend into their environment, and to create nicer public spaces. That's why you didn't see many tall buildings in Denmark till recently – they weren't considered to work very well in context.

In the past, Danish architects also exercised unusual control over a building's internal 'detailing'. When Arne

Bjarke Ingels' VM Building

Jacobsen built the Royal Hotel in Copenhagen, he also designed everything from the doorhandles to the cutlery.

"Danes are totally nuts about detailing," says Nille Juul-Sørensen, the head of the Danish Design Centre and the man who designed Copenhagen's metro stations. "We have this idea that God will see everything, even when the lights are out, behind the wall."

Bjarke Ingels changed all that. In the late 90s, Ingels worked for Rem Koolhaas, an enormously influential Dutch architect who – in very simplistic terms – believes in concept rather than context; how buildings look, rather than how they fit into their surroundings. "The street is dead," wrote Koolhaas in his 1995 book, *S, M, L, XL*. "Planning makes no difference whatsoever."

When Ingels returned to Denmark, he found that the Danish architecture scene was quite a closed shop. Big firms like CF Møller and Henning Larsen got much of the work, and it was very hard for newcomers to win contracts. Ingels and his generation realised that in order to attract business, they would have to do things differently. As a result, they followed two routes: they focussed on green, sustainable designs – and they drew significantly on the very un-Danish ideas of Koolhaas, creating buildings that are exciting in their own right, but don't sit well together.

"The first thing I read at architecture school was *Life Between Buildings*," says Dorte Mandrup, another rising star whose offices sit directly below BIG's. "But everyone was quite tired of it – this romantic, quite boring, not-so-flashy view of city life. So I think a lot of people were reacting against Jan Gehl and his sensible studies."

Ingels and his contemporaries are most famous for their work at Ørestad, the controversial new development far to the south of Copenhagen's old town. It's basically one five-kilometre-long highway, lined with humungous, eccentric, hypermodern offices and residential blocks. There's a hotel built by 3XN that looks like a massive V-sign sprouting from the ground. Two kilometres down the road, there's a giant blue box that doubles as the new home of Danish Broadcasting, and which cost so much that it sparked 300 redundancies. Further on is another futuristic cube, Ørestad High School – a sixth form without any classrooms.

Ingels has built three things here. There are the Mountain Dwellings, a sloped development that resembles a hillside made from residential flats. Next door is the VM Building, a block of flats – each stabbed by a jaunty series of knife-like balconies – that sits upon a carpark. Finally, right at the far end of Ørestad, stands the 8 Building – another high-rise that looks like a gentle rollercoaster.

You can see why they're the talk of the architectural world. There's no denying it – these are bold, fascinating sculptures. But that's also their problem: they're sculptures. They're one-offs. They look good by themselves – in a photograph or on a Powerpoint presentation – but they don't really relate to each other. In fact, they needle each other. Each feels like a stylish Porsche that someone's parked awkwardly on a kerb, and then reversed into the

Ferrari behind. Walking among them, I can't work out what they look like, or where best to view them from. It's a bit like swimming in the New York's Hudson River. You can glimpse the Empire State Building, and you can just about see the Statue of Liberty. But you can't get a good look at either, and all the while you're gulping down water – or, in Ørestad's case, car fumes. It's like drowning in architecture.

"People should definitely go out there and look at it when they come to Copenhagen," says Thomas Dickson, the author of *Dansk Design*. "But if you're thinking about it as a place to go to school or have an apartment, I don't think it's up to the best of Danish and Scandinavian traditions of how to build a neighbourhood."

It probably hasn't helped that the whole area was financed by a series of different private developers. In order to pay for the construction of a new metro system, the local government sold off bits of Ørestad to different people, all of whom wanted a unique design, but weren't so concerned about how that design related to its surroundings.

"Private clients are usually more interested in building and selling as quickly as possible, because that's where the profit is," says Mandrup. "So it's extremely market-orientated, and the market-orientated scene in architecture will always be very focussed on making it as visible as possible, and not necessarily so focussed on long-term urban life."

Ingels turned down a couple of requests for an interview. But judging from his previous statements, he would argue that Ørestad strikes exactly the right balance between concept and context.

"Architecture seems to be entrenched in two equally unfertile fronts: either naively utopian or petrifyingly pragmatic," Ingels writes in his comic, *Yes is More*. "We believe that there is a third way wedged in the no-man's-land between the diametrical opposites... A pragmatic utopian architecture that takes on the creation of socially, economically and environmentally perfect places as a practical objective."

He has his fans, too. First off, 6000 people have their homes there, a figure that looks set to triple. I can't imagine that it's the most sociable place to live – there are few shops or places to hang out – but people seem to manage. Bigwig critics have also praised the buildings. For a start, says Nille Juul-Sørensen, they're fun. "The detailing is not so good – but who cares?" he asks. "Look at the 8 Building, the VM Building. They involve you. You have to walk in funny ways to get to your flat. You can bike around, you can have your morning run inside your block. They didn't revolutionise architecture, but they changed the whole paradigm for what architecture could be."

7. AFTER THE KILLING...

"It was my ambition from the very start to do the world's best show" – Søren Sveistrup

A few kilometres north-west of Ørestad, back in the centre of Copenhagen, there's a little coffee shop called Café Holberg. Most mornings at the café, the same big-eared man sits sipping his espresso, hunched in a hoodie in the corner. If he looks suspicious, he shouldn't. He owns part of the shop. He's also Søren Malling, one of the city's most famous actors. In 2007, he played Jan Meyer, the cop who partners Sarah Lund in the first series of *The Killing*.

If this was England, the celeb-spots would end there. But this being tiny Denmark, they don't. From time to time, in walks a woman with a sharp brown bob. She lives on the same street as the café – but she's no ordinary neighbour. This is Piv Bernth, the producer of *The Killing*, and now head of drama at DR (the Danish BBC), which also puts her in overall charge of *Borgen*. If you're lucky, you might also see Sofie Gråbøl, the actor who plays Sarah Lund. She lives two streets away.

It's yet another example of the smallness of Copenhagen's creative scene. But at the same time, it shows just how big Danish TV has become. Before *The Killing*, Søren Malling wasn't particularly famous. Then he was cast as Meyer, the show went global, and a star was born. And with fame came fortune – and a stake in a coffee shop called Café Holberg.

Like Danish architecture, art, food and fashion, Danish television is on a roll. The quality of kids' TV is second to none – and then there are the crime thrillers. First came *The Killing*, in 2007 – which saw 40% (forty per cent!) of the Danish population sit down to watch Gråbøl and Malling every Sunday night. It wasn't so much a cult hit as a state religion. One day, Gråbøl was approached by the relatives of a woman dying of cancer. The woman feared she'd die before the show revealed its central secret – who killed the schoolgirl mentioned at the beginning of this book. "So I wrote her a note and put it in an envelope," Gråbøl told the *Guardian*. "She read it and tore it into little pieces so the nurse couldn't find out who did it. The following day she died."

The first two series of *The Killing* ended up on BBC4, and I visited the set of the third while it was in post-production. Around half a million Brits watched each of the earlier instalments – a startling figure for such a moody, complex, subtitled piece of Scandi noir.

"I thought: what is this?" says the show's creator, Søren Sveistrup, who was sitting with his kids by a pool in Thailand when he first heard the British viewing figures. "We're a very small country – five-point-something million – and it's impossible to make people who don't understand Danish watch our shows. It made me really proud. There were all these publishers writing to me. Could they buy *The Killing*? Was it a novel? It was kind of amazing."

Hot on the trail of *The Killing* (known in Denmark as *Forbrydelsen*, or *The Crime*) came *Borgen*, a show about a female prime minister. Odd as it may sound, this dramatisation of Scandinavian coalition politics proved an even bigger hit in Britain than *The Killing*, regularly pulling in three-quarters of a million viewers. And then there was *The Bridge*, which, with a staggering one million UK fans, was even more popular in Britain than it was in Denmark and Sweden. Each of them stars a strong woman in a position of authority – a reflection of Scandinavia's slightly more enlightened attitude to gender equality.

In *The Killing*, Sarah Lund wears the same clothes for days on end, doesn't wear make-up, and puts her work before her fiancé, mother and son – behaviour which, says Bernth, wasn't particularly surprising to a Danish audience.

"We recognise that woman," says Bernth. "She's very obsessed with her work and she wants to make a difference. And I think we kind of like that."

Overseas, Bernth notes, audiences have reacted differ-

ently – and she cites the time the German distributors doc-
tored a copy of the series poster, which shows Lund standing with her arms crossed, looking moody.

"They thought: 'Woah. God. She looks angry and boring. Ugly jumper. Woah, what do we do?' And in Photoshop
they changed her, and gave her a bra and a see-through
shirt. I was like: 'WHAT?' And so I got on my email and
stopped it immediately."

Britain took to these shows mainly because they are a)
slightly exotic; and b) simply good television: gripping, well
scripted, beautifully shot and brilliantly acted. But in
Denmark, the reasons are more complex. These three shows
are fictional, but they deal with issues that cut right to the
heart of real-life Danish politics. *Borgen*, most obviously. Its
portrayal of a female prime minister predicted the election,
in 2011, of Helle Thorning-Schmidt. The show dared to
imagine what the electorate – for all Denmark's progressive
attitudes to gender equality – had not been able to in 2007: a
woman in charge. Meanwhile, the battle Birgitte Nyborg
faces in *Borgen* to stay true to her family mirrors the real-life
experiences of Lars Løkke Rasmussen, Thorning-Schmidt's
predecessor. Halfway through his tenure, realising that he
had become estranged from his family, Rasmussen suddenly
took two weeks off to be with his children – sparking a
national debate about the responsibilities of the prime minister.

Unlike *Borgen*, *The Killing* is not exclusively a political
drama, but it is just as plugged into politics. The plot of the

second season centres on a series of small-scale terrorist attacks, apparently carried out by Muslim extremists. At first, the series implicitly questions whether these events were sparked by Denmark's aggressive role in Iraq and Afghanistan – the Danes' first acts of overseas aggression since the national catastrophe of 1864. Then, even more provocatively, the show entertains the possibility that these attacks were perpetrated not by Muslims, but by ethnic Danes. It is a plotline that seemed eerily prophetic when, two years later, the far-right activist Anders Breivik slaughtered hundreds of young Norwegians across the Baltic in Oslo.

The Killing's first series did not deal with foreign policy, but is just as deft in its treatment of domestic issues. As a police procedural, it's excellent – but the murder investigation is in many ways just a vehicle for exploring different aspects of Danish society. As old suspects prove their innocence and new ones emerge, *The Killing* moves from a portrayal of Danish family life to an analysis of Denmark's education system, before finally reaching Copenhagen city hall, and a discussion of coalition politics.

All the while, it questions Danish attitudes to immigration. One of the main characters is an Asian teacher called Rama. In a country where foreigners find it hard to fit in, Rama has done everything right: he married a Dane, he became a teacher and he fought against religious oppression. But it's still not enough. When there is the slightest, unlikeliest hint that he may somehow be involved in the murder,

Rama is immediately ostracised, even spat at by his students.

"He was well integrated," says Sveistrup. "He did what all the white guys told him to do. But when it came down to it, was he accepted? No. And that was a statement, of course. *The Killing* was a symptom of what society was. Here was a well-integrated young Asian man, who had a good job – but when hell broke loose, he got pointed at."

Airing only a year after the Muhammed cartoons crisis, Rama was right on the zeitgeist – but *The Killing* always avoided forcing a point.

"Somebody spat at the teacher," says Sveistrup. "But did that person do that because he was Asian, or because they suspected he killed the girl? I just wanted to raise the question."

For Farshad Kholghi, the actor who played Rama, the part was ground-breaking because for once it portrayed an immigrant as an engaged member of society, rather than as a gang member. Before *The Killing*, Kholghi had been so frustrated at the lack of interesting Asian parts that he wrote about the problem in his weekly column for *Jyllands-Posten*. "I said: 'Okay, I accept that you don't want me to play Hamlet or a guy called Peter or John – but why can't I play an ordinary guy named Hassan or Ali, who's a dentist, who's got a normal life, who's not a criminal?' I don't know about England, but many Iranians in Denmark are either doctors or dentists. So why I can't play the dull dentist?"

In *The Killing*, Rama was a teacher, not a dentist, but for

Kholghi he was still refreshingly normal. "It was a very cool role."

But Rama wasn't the only radical thing about *The Killing*. In fact, in production terms, the show marked a sea-change in the way that Danish television shows were made. Fifteen years ago, they simply weren't very ambitious.

"It was pretty average," says Piv Bernth, sitting in the show's studios just west of Copenhagen. "It was good for the local region but we never really made it internationally.

The Øresund: the bridge from *The Bridge*

We did a lot of plays — stage plays adapted for TV. They were very simple. They didn't have the filmic look. They were often filmed with just three cameras, which made the lights pretty boring because you had to be able to shoot from all angles." Then, in the mid-90s, Dogme happened. Championed by the likes of Lars von Trier and Thomas Winterberg, Dogme was the school of Danish cinema that focussed on narrative and pared-down aesthetics, rather than special effects. The films that were made according to Dogme's rules won widespread acclaim. Suddenly, the eyes of the film world were on Denmark.

Danish television producers were inspired – not necessarily by Dogme's specific values, but by the way Dogme had made it on the world stage. Dogme showed that Denmark, small as it was, could be a cultural force.

"We started to look at ourselves as less local and more international," says Bernth. "We became more curious and ambitious. We started travelling to the US and asking: 'Well, how do they do it?' They were so excellent, and are still so excellent, at long-running TV series. And we weren't, because we were quite new."

Bernth and her colleague Sven Clausen were at the forefront of the transition. They visited the sets of shows like *LA Law*, *NYPD Blue* and *The West Wing*, and learned about how script-writing worked for multi-episode dramas. "They had this machine going, and the 'writers' room' which was quite new to us."

The pair of them set about creating a Scandinavian version of what they had found in America. The first was Clausen's *Taxa* – a 56-episode show about the travails of a taxi company that ran for three years from 1997. This was followed in 2002 by Bernth's family drama *Nikolaj og Julie*. Both were radical for their time – but they didn't make waves outside Denmark. They were, however, the two shows on which Søren Sveistrup cut his teeth – and by the end of *Nikolaj og Julie* his reputation was so great that DR invited him to create a 20-episode crime series, based on a concept of his choosing. DR expected him to come up with something a bit like *CSI* – a show that sees a new murder solved every episode.

But Sveistrup wanted to do something a bit more ambitious – something with narrative arcs that spread over several episodes, like *Twin Peaks*, or *24*.

"I came up with the idea that the story all comes from one murder," he says. "At first, people said it couldn't be done. They said we couldn't do a story like this in 20 episodes, because people would get bored after one episode if they didn't know who the killer was."

But Sveistrup stuck to his guns, and *The Killing* was born. From the very beginning, he went about the project with the same newfound confidence that you can see in the work of other youngish Danes like Rene Redzepi, Bjarke Ingels and Claus Meyer.

"It was my ambition from the very start to do the world's best show," says Sveistrup, not in a haughty way. Tall, pale, and softly-spoken, he communicates with a quiet authority that never approaches arrogance. "People laughed at me. They said, 'Oh, we can't do that, we're only Danish.' Which is typically Danish. We're not boasting types. But I wanted to do something exceptional. I was fed up with people saying that television is just television. We all watch feature films on our television screens – and the same stuff that you tell in those feature films, you could also tell in a television show."

He achieved this not just through *The Killing*'s structure, but in the way it was shot. "Typical television is just close-ups. There would be a close-up with you and then a close-up with me. Talking heads. But I wanted to make it more epic – visually more epic. Larger pictures. Spaghetti western stuff. We often talked about westerns, actually. I've seen Clint Eastwood's films many times. One man would arrive on a train. Another man would just look at him, and between them they'd create a moment. I still use that example to remind me not to get too busy with dialogue. Remember the pictures. Always the pictures. And the characters. Sarah Lund is the silent type. She didn't need to say much. I hated detectives when they talked about their private lives. Clint Eastwood is the mysterious type. He doesn't talk much. He's silent – and because he's silent, we have to imagine all kinds of stuff going on in his mind."

He may have had his doubters, but Sveistrup had the last laugh. It's subjective, of course, but *The Killing* is considered one of the world's best television shows since *The Wire*. Bernth says it paved the way for later Scandi series like *The Bridge*, which wasn't made by DR, but follows a similar structure to *The Killing*, and features an introverted female lead who draws comparisons to Sarah Lund.

"Everybody said we were crazy," says Bernth. "They said we weren't going to get the audience, because people wouldn't want to sit there every Sunday and wait for 20 weeks to get the killer. But they did. It became an obsession. And I think *The Bridge* was very much inspired by that."

The Killing also broke ground simply through the size of its cast across the (soon-to-be) three seasons. The Danish acting community isn't especially large – and you constantly see the same actors in different shows. On the wall of a room at *The Killing* studios, there's a photo of Peter Mygind and Sofie Gråbøl. The photo is a still from *Nicolai og Julie*, in which the two actors starred. Tellingly, both of them would go on to play lead roles in, respectively, *Borgen* and *The Killing*. Søren Malling has big roles in both *The Killing* and *Borgen*, as do Bjarne Henriksen and Mikael Birkkjaer. Meanwhile, Kim Bodnia, who plays Martin Rohde in *The Bridge*, also has a part in *The Killing*. This list of crossovers goes on and on – and it prompted the *Guardian* to run a

Súsan Johansen: the woman who knitted *that* jumper

Venn diagram of them all under a headline that asked: "Has Denmark run out of actors?"

Can this be true? I ask Bernth. Not quite, she laughs. But because she has a policy of not recycling actors, *The Killing* has got through 400 of them – "which is a lot for Denmark". Mikael Birkkjaer, who plays Lund's mysterious partner in the second series, very nearly didn't get the part because he'd played such a different role as the prime minister's academic husband in *Borgen*. "We originally said: 'No, we don't want Mikael, he's just been a doctor for 20 episodes.' But he was the best and he was the one who had the connection with Sofie."

By now Bernth and I are touring the set. First we pop through the editing suites, where – on a huge Apple screen – Sarah Lund has just woken up in a hotel bed in Jutland. "Episode six of the new series," says Bernth. We move on, through a vast white hangar where once stood the home of Nanna Birk Larsen, the murdered schoolgirl, and then we're suddenly inside a police station. We could be in a scene of *The Killing 2* – after all, we just walked past the actor who plays Brix, Lund's boss. But there's one key difference: the place, so pristine in the earlier series, is now a tip. The mirrors are smashed; there's debris everywhere. It's a symptom of one of the themes for the new series: the financial crisis, and the effect it's having on state institutions like the police force.

Sveistrup says that once again he's using the series to tap into current political debate. During the first two series,

Denmark was consumed with a conversation about race and identity – and *The Killing* reflected that. Now the national debate has changed. It's concerned with the economy, and, accordingly, so is *The Killing*.

"Before the financial crisis, we had a fight of values," he says. "Western values versus the foreigners, the immigrants. Is it okay to wear a scarf at work? There was a big discussion about that kind of thing. But not any more. The financial crisis has taken centre stage. Everything has turned into a conversation about money – and I'm going with it."

He's tight-lipped about the details, but from what I can make out, the third series centres on a rich mogul whose family member is kidnapped. Is he based on Mærsk Mc-Kinney, the Danish shipping tycoon? "I can't remember," deadpans a grinning Sveistrup. And what about the jumpers? Will Sarah Lund wear yet another bit of knitwear? Sveistrup just smiles.

•

Súsan Johansen knits with the nonchalance of a teenager sending a text. Her needles click furiously through the yarn heaped in her lap – but apart from the occasional downward glance, her gaze is directed elsewhere. At her coffee, at passing bikes, at me. A social worker by profession, the knitting is just something she does on her way to work. Which is unexpected, because for many people – particularly the millions who watch *The Killing* – her knitting has reached cult status. From the very first episode, Sarah Lund wears a feminised fisherman's jumper – creamy white, skin-tight, and ringed with a row of large black snowflakes. Episode after episode, Lund never seems to take it off – and pretty soon viewers wanted to copy her. The *Radio Times* ran a feature called, "How to knit your own Sarah Lund jumper." The *Guardian* had "Sarah Lund's jumper – explained." There's even a website devoted to it: SarahLundSweater. com, which tells you both where to buy the original and where to head for cheaper knock-offs. The real thing is from the Faroes, a splattering of islands in the far north of the Atlantic that technically belong to Denmark. It was designed by the small fashion house Gudrun and Gudrun, and Johansen is the middle-aged Faroese woman who first knitted it. Sitting in front of me now, at a table outside Kalaset café in central Copenhagen, she is about to knit another one.

"Nobody knew that this strange jumper would eventually get so much attention," remembers Gudrun Rógvadóttir, the business half of Gudrun and Gudrun. In the mid-2000s, homespun knitwear was out of fashion. In the Faroes, local wool was burnt as a waste product when the islands' sheep were sent to slaughter. Horrified, Gudrun Rógvadóttir, a former consultant, joined forces with Gudrun Ludvig, a local designer, and the pair set out to revitalise the dying art of the Faroese fisherman's jumper.

The jumper goes back a long way in the Faroes, a place where fishing and sheep-herding still play a role in local life. There are similar jumpers in Iceland, but there the colours are brighter, and the patterns are rounder. In the 1800s, says

Rógvadóttir, each Faroese village would have had their own unique designs.

"At that time, all healthy men over 14 went to sea in the old boats," she tells me, on the phone from the Faroese capital, Torshavn. "They all went away in springtime, and they didn't come back until autumn, and in that time there was no communication between the fishermen and their families." On their return, the villagers would gather on the shore to watch the boats sail in from the horizon – and to see which fishermen had returned safely. "Everybody knew that every year the sea would take some of the fishermen. And the story goes that the patterns on the sweaters were so special, and so clear, that even before the face of the man could be seen, you'd be able to identify them by the patterns on the sweater. So all of a sudden the patterns could tell the difference between life and death."

By the 1970s, the Faroese sweater carried a different symbolism. "It was really big in the hippy period," says fashion designer Henrik Vibskov. "For some people, the sweater was a symbol of a day off. Nature. Walking at the beach. My brother and sister were hanging out in these sweaters, wearing the Palestinian scarf, with hippy long hair."

Sofie Gråbøl, who plays Sarah Lund, also remembers wearing the jumper during her hippyish upbringing. She says that it symbolises *hygge*, the Danish concept explored in earlier chapters that translates badly into English as "cosy" or "togetherness". "That sweater," Gråbøl has said, "was a sign of believing in togetherness."

But by the late 90s, many local women had stopped knitting, and the tradition looked to be dying out. Gudrun Ludvig decided to do something about it.

"She took a sweater of her dad's," says Rógvadóttir. "And her thought was to simplify it. The old ones were very thick, made for fishermen – but she wanted to adapt the sweater so that it could be used by a woman, a mother. Altered to be so small that you could wear it inside a small jacket."

Ludvig knew Súsan Johansen through her sister, and she knew that she knitted. So she brought Johansen the snowflake pattern and asked her to make a jumper from it. It took a week of back-and-forth before Johansen, who was used to making baggier shapes, realised what Ludvig wanted.

"She kept saying: 'Make it smaller, make it smaller'," says Johansen.

She got there eventually, and in 2007 the two Gudruns took the range to the Copenhagen fashion show. One day, a producer from DR turned up and said they were working on a TV series and they were looking for some clothing. The producer took two jumpers, and later asked the firm to send some more. "And then we didn't hear anything until the series was on two years later. Suddenly there was a lot of talk about the sweater. After a couple of episodes, the papers started saying: 'Is she going to wear this sweater all this time? Doesn't she have any other clothing? What is that sweater?' The whole story was about the sweater."

Johansen is slightly non-plussed about it all. "It was very funny," she says. "Everyone was saying: 'You made Sarah Lund's jumper'." But she's kept herself grounded. She was proud to see her work on screen, but she didn't watch all the episodes. She helped make the red jumper Lund wears in the second series, but she didn't like it so much – "Too Icelandic!", she says. Three years ago she moved to Copenhagen, and still knits three jumpers a week for Gudrun and Gudrun. She orders the wool from certain Faroese farms and gets friends to carry back the finished products. She says knitting stops her smoking – something to keep her hands busy when she's on the train to the care home where she works. She's even started teaching her patients to knit.

But Johansen is no longer the jumper's sole knitter. Gudrun and Gudrun employ around 60 knitters – mostly in the Faroes, but some in Jordan, where Rógvadóttir used to work – and each will specialise in a specific size range.

"No two people knit in completely the same way," explains Rógvadóttir. Someone might knit particularly tightly, in which case they're asked to make small sizes. "If someone has a slightly looser hand, we'll make them a medium. But the difficult thing is that the same woman can knit a small one day, and the next day she'll knit a medium. If you are very relaxed, you'll knit looser. But if you're stressed, you'll knit smaller and more tightly. Maybe your husband was stupid that day, so you'll knit tighter. It's very emotional and personal."

It's important not to overstate the knitting resurgence in Scandinavia: one class of sixth-formers I talk to groan when I mention that jumper. But there is definitely something going on. Since 2006, Gudrun and Gudrun's profits have increased more than tenfold (though Rógvadóttir is at pains to emphasise that they're about so much more than just jumpers.)

"The whole handcraft thing has completely blown up," says Vibskov. "It's become something. Nowadays, everything goes so fast – you know, the World Wide Web, click click click – so people are trying to hook onto something more stable, old-school."

It's not just thanks to *The Killing*, either. On the other side of town, halfway towards the airport, half a dozen elderly women are knitting in the garden of an old people's day centre. The oldest is 96, the youngest 65. The chattiest, Ketty Brøgger, was 80 last week. They natter away, sipping on coffee, munching on homemade cakes. They are the ladies of Kaffeslabberas, a knitting group for pensioners. They could be any gaggle of grannies, but to the fashion-conscious Dane, they are almost minor celebrities, and their story has also played an unlikely role in the revival of Danish wool.

It all started when Susanne Hoffmann, one of Henrik Vibskov's designers, had her first baby. While on maternity leave, she got lonely. Cooped up at home in suburban Amager, south-east Copenhagen, she was cut off from her friends across town in trendy Vesterbro. Then she found an unlikely salvation: Sløjfen, the local pensioners' club. There were always things happening there – workshops, stalls, afternoon bingo – and Hoffmann wondered whether they'd want to start a knitting club. No one responded to her initial advert on the noticeboard, so one day she ambled in with an armful of yarn and asked if anyone wanted to join her. Around ten women did, and they started meeting every Tuesday lunchtime. *Kaffeslabberas* – which roughly means "coffee table chat" – was born.

At first, it was purely about the company. "They're very wise," says Hoffmann, under a canopy in the garden. "They gave me advice about being a mother." But then she asked if they might knit some baby jumpers for her baby son. Maybe, they said – never ones to be dictated to. "But then a week later, they'd suddenly done it all. I was amazed at the quality. They were so fast."

Impressed, she told her boss about her new friends, and eventually Vibskov came down to see what the fuss was about. He liked what he saw – "and so Susie was like, 'Hey, Henrik, why don't we sell some of this down at the shop?'" And so they did – baby sweaters at first, and then scarves. Before long. a huge high-street designer called Mads Nørgaard had heard about the group, and wanted in. So they started making him a few socks every month – long grey stockings with a ring of red at the top – and donated all the profits back to their club. Then everything snowballed. All of a sudden, *Kaffeslabberas* were the fashion world's plaything du jour. They staged knitting performances in the windows of a shop in central Copenhagen. They were interviewed on national television, and given ringside seats at the capital's biggest fashion show – much to their bafflement.

"We all lined up and knitted during the show while the photographers were lying around us trying to take our picture," a bewildered Brøgger told one newspaper. "They were putting all their best dresses on," remembers Vibskov. Affectionately, he adopts the shrill voice of a pensioner: "Ewnewnew. The music is very loud. Awahhh. Is that a famous person over there? Famous!"

A book of their work followed – fittingly, a big coffee table tome – but all the while the group kept on meeting every week for cake, coffee and a good old gossip. Like Johansen, they find the interest in their work hilarious – not least because these are the same designs that their grandchildren were only recently so snooty about.

"I can't understand it," laughs 86-year-old Lily Nielsen. "People pay so much. We always made these things for our children and now people are paying us 250 kroner [around £30] for them."

8. JUTLAND:
happiness country?

"We're not hippies…This is a business like any other business" – Søren Hermansen

Denmark looks quite odd on a map. Its capital is on an island called Sjælland that is so far east, it's almost in Sweden. Further west lies Fyn, a smallish blob that houses Odense, and the childhood home of Hans Christian Andersen. To the left of Fyn, there's Jylland, or Jutland – the biggest bit of Denmark, and the only part attached to mainland Europe. It lives up to its anglicised name, jutting like a mohawk from Germany's northern border. Halfway up Jutland's western coast – about as far from Copenhagen as you can possibly travel in Denmark – is a little town called Ringkøbing. It's a pretty town, too. Small, pretty buildings squashed between a lagoon and a quaint town square – and all 15 minutes from the sand dunes and summer houses that skirt the North Sea.

According to a no doubt unerringly accurate survey of residents by Cambridge University, Ringkøbing is the happiest town in Denmark. And given that Denmark is consistently named by the UN as the world's happiest country, this technically makes Ringkøbing – pop: 9000 – the happiest town on earth. In pursuit of happiness, and hoping for a taste of Jutland, I head to Ringkøbing for the weekend. The journey takes three train legs, and so by the time I arrive, it's nearly midnight. The streets are dark, the air is silent, and there is no one in sight. It's deserted. If this is happiness, I feel very short-changed. But suddenly a noise flies over the rooftops. It's the sound of shouting and, thinking it might just also be the sound of happiness, I head in its general direction. Following my ear, I weave through the backstreets of Ringkøbing, and with every step the sounds get louder. At last, I'm almost there. Just one more turning, and I'll have reached nirvana itself.

I round the corner. I look up.

Screaming at the top of their lungs, three drunk teenagers are pissing against a wall.

•

I could be in any small town on a Friday night – and for their part, my new friends are keen to dispel any myths about the place. Excited to meet someone new, they invite me back to their den, a shed that sits at the bottom of their friend's nearby garden. Sobering up, they tell me a tale of provincial teenage angst. There's only one bar in town, they say – not that there's anyone they want to see there. "We're in a minority in this town," says Oscar, 17 last month, and "still very, very excited about it." He and his friends Klaus, Alexander and Asbjørn are creative types, he says. They write poetry. They play music. Unlike their sporty neighbours, they go to a continuation school that focuses on drama and art. "We're very rare in Ringkøbing," he sighs. "It's not that usual for people in Jylland to write and be creative. There are a lot of people who just ride about and drink alcohol." And with that, he pops out for another piss.

The next day, I visit the town's local newspaper, the *Ringkøbing-Skjern Dagbladet*. The staff there are not nearly as down on the town, but back in 2007, they too were surprised to find it was the happiest place on earth.

"We really were astonished," says the paper's jovial chief reporter, a small middle-aged man called Poul Osmundsen. "Later, we tried to find out on what statistical basis they had reached their conclusion. The material was rather skimpy. Statistically speaking, it was totally invalid. But it went totally viral. Before we knew it, we were being visited by television crews from all over the world. I have to say, the townspeople were rather bemused by it. Most of us have had many good laughs about it. One of the local traits is modesty. We do not regard ourselves as something special. So all this exposure was something quite unfamiliar."

But it got the townsfolk thinking, Poul remembers. "It made us reflect. If we are the happiest town in the world, why would that be? And I don't think it's totally faulty. I do think people here are... well, happy is the wrong word. That means giddy, or exultant, or a rather fleeting emotion. The right term would be 'contented'. We are a contented society."

The gap between the richest and poorest is very small in Ringkøbing, says Osmundsen – even by Danish standards. "We all attend the same schools, the same sports clubs, the same shops. We live, more or less, in the same neighbourhood." In other words, no one has it much better than anyone else.

As a result, the people of Ringkøbing are happy with what they've got – a quality which, people constantly tell me, puts them at odds with snobbish Copenhageners.

"We see ourselves as very different to Copenhageners," says Peter Donslund, a senior civil servant at the town hall. "In Copenhagen they spend much more money, but here people are much more satisfied. Our attitude is not so much for complaining here." Perhaps that's why the area votes en masse for Venstre, whose business-friendly policies appeal to an entrepreneurial local population used to doing things by themselves.

"We think that we work harder," says Osmundsen. "We think that we are better, that we are more frugal. We are country mice and they are city mice. They talk much faster – too much in some cases."

It's a tension that the anthropologist Richard Jenkins explores (and to some extent debunks) in his book, *Being Danish*. To illustrate the Jutland reserve, Jenkins retells a well-known joke about a Jutland farmer interviewing a new labourer. The farmer looks at the young man and says, "I suppose you'll do. But there's one thing you should know. We don't do too much talking here. We just get on with the work." The young man nods, and starts work immediately. A year later, the farmer approaches the man again and tells him that he's thinking of buying a new bicycle. The labourer nods, and goes back to work. Six months on, the farmer mentions to him that he's just bought the bike he was talking about half a year previously. Again, the labourer nods, and gets on with what he was doing. Yet another six months go by, and this time it's the labourer's turn to approach the farmer. "I'm sorry," he says, "but I'm going to have to leave." The farmer's surprised. "What's up?" he asks. "Don't I pay you enough?" "No, it's not that," says the young man. "But I can't stand any more of this bicycle talk."

It's an exaggeration, of course – but the joke highlights the difference between the hard-working, taciturn Jutlanders and the chatty, lazy Copenhageners. "How can you find the Jutlander in Copenhagen?" begins another Jutland joke. "Just ask to see the boss."

Yet for all their superiority, the people I meet in Ringkøbing feel a profound sense of inferiority, or at least abandonment. "Copenhagen people think this is a backwater," says a doleful Oscar. "They stereotype us as fishermen. They think we're peasants and rednecks. But they're people who just think about how they look."

The abandonment has physical manifestations, too. Everyone claims that state funding has been siphoned away from west Jutland and towards Copenhagen, or even Aarhus, Jutland's eastern capital. Under the last government, political decision-making also became more centralised. Ringkøbing was stripped of its position as the seat of the regional government, while decisions about local housing construction were made from Copenhagen – a move which made west Jutlanders feel angry and helpless. Meanwhile, Ringkøbing sits in the centre of a (relatively) deprived area of Denmark known back in Copenhagen as the "rotten banana". A strip that runs from north-west Jutland, down its western flank, and then east along the south of Fyn, the banana is home to rising unemployment and lacks centres of higher education.

It's a situation at odds with the role Jutland has played in Denmark's history. In a way, you could argue that Jutland represents Denmark's soul. It was here that the first cooperatives took off, where the first folk high schools were built, and it was the farmers from here who, in the 1890s, pushed through parliament the first steps towards a Danish welfare state. And though Copenhageners are said to be snobby about Jutland, everyone likes to claim their family was originally from here. We're a nation of farmers, Copenhageners will proudly tell you – and this helps to explain why Ringkøbing might still be so contented. Whatever else has happened since, locals know that their part of the world is the source of Denmark's founding myths. "Jutland," as Richard Jenkins summarises so neatly in his book, "is both centre and periphery within the Danish historical narrative, a place of backward obscurity and the wellspring of enlightenment."

Danes often talk about how much they trust each other, and how, whatever *The Killing* might suggest, their country has a relatively low crime rate. In practice, it's difficult to estimate how trusting Denmark is – but there's certainly a lot of it in Ringkøbing. "It's a secure community," says Bent Brodersen, a local councillor for Venstre, and a man once named by French TV as the world's happiest man. "We don't fear for crime, terror, wild animals, monsoon."

"People usually don't cheat each other," says Else Mathiassen, headteacher at the West Jutland folk high school, down the road from Ringkøbing. "For instance, my daughter lost her purse. She was sure it would come back to her. She didn't even get nervous. And it did get back to her! She knew it would be delivered to the police station. And it was! She didn't know where she lost it. She's done it several times. Once in a taxi. Another time by a bus stop. And it always got back to her."

It doesn't really need to be said, but the town has a strong sense of community. Everyone is part of a club – at a funding meeting at the town hall recently, representatives from 60 clubs turned up. That's at least 60 clubs for a town of only 9000 citizens. The old-fashioned local bank – Ringkøbing Landbobank – is one of the country's most stable. "Stinginess is traditionally a local trait," says

Osmundsen. "And well, some people say the bank has this same trait."

Meanwhile the continued success of Osmundsen's own employers – the *Ringkøbing-Skjern Dagbladet* – speaks of a community that cares about its local institutions. Unlike local newspapers in Britain, the *Dagbladet* hasn't been decimated by redundancies, their advertising revenues have held up well, and, most indicatively, their circulation remains a steady 8500 – not bad for a county with less than 60,000 residents. "Our readers are very loyal," says Lars Kryger, the paper's chief subeditor, munching on a very sugary slice of cake. "They feel that if we were not here, something would be missing. They know we're a cornerstone in this town's life."

Another secret to Ringkøbing's contentedness lies in its relative lack of racial tension. "There is no talk of immigration or integration," claims Donslund. "People don't talk about foreigners as part of a group, but more like every other citizen. It's a special thing about this area." This is partly because there aren't many immigrants. In the 70s, when many people arrived from Turkey and Pakistan, they moved to areas where there was a large textile industry – something not present in Ringkøbing.

There are nevertheless two groups of foreign communities – one Iraqi, the other Bosnian. But unlike many other immigrants I meet in Denmark, the ones in Ringkøbing seem genuinely at home. At the Danish-Bosnian Community Centre, behind a petrol station on the outskirts of town, I chat to a Bosnian Muslim called Damir Zvirkic, whom we met briefly in Chapter five. He loves Denmark, perhaps because the 400 Bosnians in Ringkøbing were – by his account – part of a group granted asylum in 1993 after a personal intervention from Margrethe, the Danish queen. Zvirkic feels Danish now, even – as he mentions earlier – when he goes back to Bosnia on holiday. He says that it helps that Bosnians aren't particularly fervent Muslims, and so find it easier to become part of the community.

"People from Yugoslavia and Bosnia generally want to integrate. And Danish people like it when they see people trying to integrate. If you're trying, there's no problem. I'm trying – and I think sometimes it is enough to try."

Certainly, the attendance at the Danish-Bosnian Community Centre suggests he's right. It's bingo night, and it's not just Bosnians writing down numbers – around a third of the club's members are ethnic Danes.

Ringkøbing has one further secret. Jobs. It may lie at the core of the rotten banana, but the town hasn't been hit by the banana's worst problem: spiralling unemployment. Before the financial crisis, unemployment here was at 1%, one of the lowest rates in Denmark. Post-2008, it's still only at 3.5% – one reason why immigrants are still absorbed into the community without a grumble. It's all down to the area's surprisingly wide economic base, which creates a lot of jobs for skilled and non-skilled workers alike. First, there's the cattle industry, still one of the country's largest. Then there's the metalworks – per capita, this is Denmark's most industrial area. The tourist trade is also booming – the summer houses on the dunes of the North Sea have long been a favourite summer haunt for both Germans and Danes. And finally, there's Ringkøbing's most famous son: Vestas, the world's biggest windmill-maker. They've now moved their headquarters east to Aarhus and cut their workforce here from 2500 to 2200, but their presence is still felt economically – and visually. Wherever you turn, in the distance you can always see a long line of rotating turbines – a constant reminder that you're in one of the greenest countries in the world.

•

Erik Andersen does not look like a man of the future. His hair is white, he's 66, and his cheeks are grooved by crows' feet. Hair mushrooms from his ears. His cat sleeps on the window-sill, and in the corner a grandfather clock – handed down from his parents – ticks the tock of decades past.

But looks deceive. If you step outside Andersen's farmhouse and squint towards the southern horizon – south of the mill-pond, south of his herd of rare Red Danish cows – you will see a slim line of windmills. When the wind's up, they cartwheel across the fields like ballet dancers in slow motion. When the breeze stops, they stand like Greek heroes resting on their shields.

We're on the tiny island of Samsø, a few kilometres east of Jutland, and these windmills – which belong in part to Andersen – have made Samsø one of the largest carbon-neutral settlements on the planet, and the doyen of the green world. Søren Hermansen, the local teacher who spearheaded the island's green movement, remembers visiting New York for the first time a few years ago. He was eating out with his wife. The waiter – realising they were Danish – said he'd just read an article about Danish windmills in the *New Yorker*. "He said the writer had been to this little island called Samsø. Had we heard of it?"

Fifteen years ago, Samsø's 4000 elderly farmers were known best for their early crop of new potatoes. Their farms were all powered by fossil fuels, which had to be shipped over from the mainland, and between them they created 45,000 tons of carbon dioxide each year. Then, in 1998, all that changed. These conservative islanders were the unlikely winners of a competition to become Denmark's first carbon-neutral community. Government funding followed – an investment matched by the islanders themselves – and a decade and a half later, 10 offshore windmills line the coast of Samsø, while 11 stud its fields.

Many farmers – Andersen included – have layered their roofs with solar panels. Their heating, once organised on an individual basis, now comes from a central supplier – which cuts down on waste – and is created from burning straw. Some of their plumbing – at the island's Energy Academy, for instance – even runs on rainwater. "The water may look brown," warns a sign next to their toilets.

The upshot is that Samsø isn't just carbon neutral – it's technically carbon negative. The energy Samsingers can't use is fed back into the Danish national grid, which means that their net output of carbon dioxide stands at -15,000 tons. And they're not stopping there. By 2030, they don't just want to offset their tractors' use of petrol: they want to stop using fossil fuels altogether. To do this, they want everyone to trade in their cars for electric ones. But they've got a long way to go. A jungle of rentable bicycles may greet you when you step off the ferry, but they're not particularly useful on an island that still takes half an hour to cross by car. Meanwhile, electric cars are unaffordable to many, and – if my taxi driver's pained expression was anything to go by – most Samsingers still need to be persuaded of their appeal.

Historically, they've been won over by arguments of an economic bent. Five of the turbines are owned by the council, 12 by individual farmers, but, most significantly, four are managed cooperatively by hundreds of locals. Erik Andersen is one of them. Back in the late 90s, he invested £6000 of his own savings in the cooperative turbines. Six years later, he'd made it back, and now he turns a healthy profit every year. "There's money in it," he smiles. "It's a good investment."

Samsø isn't an anomaly in Denmark. In general, the country has made one of the sincerest attempts to tackle climate change. Since 1980, their economy has grown by 70%, while, staggering, their electricity usage has stayed the same. Copenhagen wants to become the world's first carbon-neutral capital by 2025, and they'll probably get there – if Aarhus doesn't beat them to it. To smooth the way, the state government has introduced a 180% tax on car sales. An integrated public transport system also helps, as does all that cycling infrastructure. Then there's the district heating system, which heats around 60% of Danish houses centrally.

The Danes are good at recycling too. Denmark produces proportionally more waste than any other country in Europe, but just five per cent of it ends up in landfill. In the US, that figure rises to 54%. Meanwhile, Danish law demands that buildings be much better insulated than they are in other countries. As a result, Danish architects invest heavily in finding new ways of keeping buildings warm. When I visit the offices of 3XN, I see boxes of maize, cotton, cork and flax – mushrooms, even – the residue of a quest to find the perfect way to insulate a house. "It's really funny when you go abroad and British architects talk about sustainability," says Dorte Mandrup, one of the rising stars of Danish architecture. "It means something completely different."

But the biggest thing is wind power. Look out of almost any window in Denmark and you'll see a flat countryside flecked with white turbines. They're the world's largest producers of windmills. Twenty per cent of Danish energy comes from wind, and by 2020, they hope it'll be 50%. By 2030, they want to be rid of fossil fuels altogether, replacing them with both biomass plants, and yet more bigger, better wind turbines. British criticism of wind power centres on its ugliness and its inefficiency. But when I get talking to one of

Vestas's lead engineers I chance upon in a bar in Aarhus, he rubbishes both claims. Vestas, he claims, are developing a kind of gargantuan, floating wind farm that will be a) so far out to sea that you won't be able to see it (thus placating those who don't like the look of a sleek white windmill); and b) so windy that it'll able to power half the world. In the meantime, he says, Vestas are about to release their largest turbine yet. With a wingspan of 172m, it'll be effective even in countries that aren't as flat as Denmark, and don't have as much wind.

Accurate or not, his passion shows how seriously Denmark takes green energy. But contrary to popular belief, this isn't because Danes are eco-warriors. "We're not hippies," says Søren Hermansen. As explained in Chapter six, Danish environmentalism is pragmatic rather than idealistic. In the 70s, Denmark was particularly hard hit by the oil crisis, which made Danes anxious to find a long-term replacement for fossil fuel. With all their flat land, wind

power seemed a sensible option.

First of all, it makes sense from an economic perspective. "This is business like any other business," says Hermansen, who I chat to on the ferry over from the mainland. "If we can provide cheap energy to compete with fossil fuel, then even the most conservative local citizen will say green energy is good. It is more reliable and cheaper, because we can see our prices going up all the time. When we started in 1998, oil was $30 per barrel. Ten years later, it was $130. So the people who invested between 1998 and 2001 saved so much money in the next ten years. We could show that this was a real business project, not just a hippy project."

A change in the way that government subsidies are structured has also helped speed up the process. A few decades ago, the government wanted to encourage turbine construction, so they gave grants to the factories themselves. "But they found this didn't improve the quality of turbines," says Hermansen. "Manufacturers produced rubbish wind turbines and still survived." During the 90s, the government took away this subsidy and gave it to the people who bought the turbines instead. They agreed to buy back any unused wind energy from the turbine owners at a price that never dropped below a fixed minimum. This encouraged communities to invest in turbines that created the most power – and in turn prompted the manufacturers themselves to create better turbines.

Wind's success is also down, once again, to the cooperative system that is so engrained in the Danish way of life. In

Britain, local communities have often been opposed to windmills because they see them as thrust upon a particular area by external forces. In Denmark, it's usually the locals who have built and paid for them, and who have decided where they're sited. There are around 6000 turbines in Denmark (nearly double the number in Britain, a country 6 times its size) and around 75% of them are co-owned by around 150,000 Danes. It's these people, not the large energy companies, who most profit from the lowered energy bills, and from the sales of excess energy back to the national grid. As a result, even the most conservative locals have invested, both financially and emotionally, in the turbines – even a bunch of elderly, grizzled farmers in the middle of the North Sea.

It's a very Danish situation. "In England, you are a coal nation," says Hermansen, as the ferry pulls towards Samsø. "The British empire was fuelled by coal. But in Denmark, we are a farming nation, and so everything has historically been decided by co-ops. The co-op structure has been around for 150 years, and it's still going strong."

A line of turbines glide past our ferry window.

"This isn't a coincidence," says Hermansen. "It couldn't have happened in any other place."

EPILOGUE

In May 2011, a sociologist called Ulla Holm wrote an article for *Politiken* about the New Nordic kitchen. It was an explosive piece. Holm claimed that chefs like Rene Redzepi – with their focus on local produce and their desire to create a regional culinary identity – were closet nationalists. Nordic supremacists, even. "It is hardly a coincidence," she wrote, "that the waiters were dressed in brown shirts when I last visited Noma."

Her argument was bonkers. As Claus Meyer explains earlier in this book, the New Nordic mission is utterly innocent. It's simply about making people more interested in good, sustainable food. And it's a global aim, he points out, not just a Scandinavian one.

"Look at my family. My father's a Muslim immigrant. My wife, Nadine, is Jewish," Redzepi told the *New Yorker*. "If the supremacists took over, we'd be out of here."

Yet in a funny, roundabout way, Holm's article touches

on something fundamental to contemporary Denmark. She's wrong about Noma, but the tension she erroneously sees between the restaurant's ambition and its parochialism is one that is nevertheless very present within wider Danish life. For the last 150 years, Denmark has – with several notable exceptions – hidden itself away. But in the past two decades, the country has increasingly found that this coping mechanism no longer works in a globalised world. Denmark is and can no longer be a monoculture.

Danes have reacted to this challenge in ways that contradict each other – some parochial, others ambitious. And as Richard Jenkins notes in his book, *Being Danish*, the direction they will ultimately take remains to be seen.

One direction is inwards and backwards. Many Danes can see the world on their doorstep, and they're trying to keep it out. They want to preserve the Danish identity, but in the process of doing so, they have ironically eroded it. By virtually ending immigration, and by attempting to stamp out the individuality of immigrant communities, groups like the Dansk Folkeparti have forgone the tolerant and democratic values that supposedly form the backbone of Danishness.

Another direction is outwards. Some Danes have seen the world outside – and want to conquer it. Some have done this aggressively: for the first time since 1864, Danish soldiers have been in action abroad, as part of the peacekeeping force in Iraq and Afghanistan. Others are trying to take over the world in a more creative sense. As this book has shown,

Danes like Søren Sveistrup, Rene Redzepi and Bjarke Ingels are some of the best in the world in their respective fields. Through their success, they have reinforced Danish culture – Redzepi, for instance, has helped to revitalise Danish food – but, like their isolationist countrymen, they too have also changed what it is to be Danish. Increasingly their influences are international – Sveistrup looked to the US, Ingels to Holland – and their heightened ambition is at odds with the traditional image of a contented, laid-back Dane.

It's hard to say which of these directions Denmark will eventually settle on. Perhaps it'll be all of them. But whichever it is, one thing is fairly certain: the concept of Danishness is changing. How to be Danish is hard enough to explain in 2012. How to be Danish in two decades' time is anyone's guess.

THE GREAT DANES

7 - name of the Arne Jacobsen chair that inspired Christine Keeler's semi-nude portrait

£11.40 - average per hour minimum wage in Denmark

1000 - number of people on the waiting list at Noma most nights

96% - percentage of children aged 3–5 in state-subsidised daycare

3% - percentage of Danes who are Muslim

4% - percentage of Danes called Larsen

74% - approximate percentage of Danish mothers in work

1901 - the last time any party won an overall majority

54,700 kroner - average lawyer's salary

34,400 kroner - average binman's salary

1200 - number of stitches in a Fritz Hansen Egg chair

0 kroner - cost of university tuition

173m - height of Jutland's Yding Skovhøj, the highest point in Denmark

20% - percentage of electricity powered by wind

26% - percentage of children aged 7–14 with part-time jobs

400 - number of actors who appeared in The Killing

2004 - year New Nordic cuisine was founded

36% - percentage of Copenhageners who commute by bike

15 - number of ways in which Erwin Lauterbach can prepare celery, according to Bent Christensen

14 - total number of Michelin stars in Denmark

9.1% - percentage of Danish residents who are of an immigrant background

26 - years in which an immigrant must have lived in Denmark in order for them to marry a non-EU citizen

1962 - year Jan Gehl spent studying Copenhagen's first "walking street"

406 - number of Danish islands

98% - percentage of Copenhagen homes connected to district heaters

60 - number of knitters employed by Gudrun and Gudrun, the makers of Sarah Lund's jumper

2025 - year by which Copenhagen hopes to be the world's first carbon-neutral capital

40% - percentage of the Danish population who watched the first series of The Killing

7314 - kilometres of Danish coastline

ACKNOWLEDGEMENTS

I'm aware that I'm about to thank a lot of people – but the truth is that, directly or indirectly, a lot of people helped me write this book.

In particular, I want to thank my publishers, Aurea Carpenter and Rebecca Nicolson – and their colleague Dave Isaacs. I wouldn't be anywhere without my parents, Jenny and Stephen, and my brother Tom. I am also indebted to Tom, Daniel Cohen, Emma Hogan, Lars Hinnerskov Eriksen, Karoline Kirchhübel Andersen, Anne-Lise Kjaer, Sarah Parkes and Elliot Ross – all of whom read significant chunks of the manuscript at various stages.

I'm equally grateful to my Danish teacher, Alette Scales, and her husband Alan. Before I left, I received some great advice from Kasper Fogh, Lone Britt Christensen and Kirsten Syppli Hansen. In Denmark itself, I was amazed by the generosity of Mouns Overgaard, Dorte Lec Fischer, Troels Leth Petersen, Astrid Lindhardt, Bi Skaarup, Susanne Hoffmann, Jørgen Halskov, Annemarie Zinck, Winnie and Thomas Kongshaug, Steen Sauerberg, Sandra Hoj, Charlotte Rye, Martin Kirchhübel, Gitte Lehrmann, Carl Valentin, Søren Witte, Rikke Bech, Nancy Frich, Kanar Patruss and Chris Scales.

At Short, I thank Catherine Gibbs and Clemmie Jackson Stops – and Katherine Stroud, who publicised the book. Karoline Kirchhübel Andersen drew the splendid illustrations.

Elsewhere, I doubt I'd ever have written this book without the faith and guidance of so many people at the Guardian. Thank you: Suzie Worroll, Malik Meer, Emily Wilson, Clare Margetson, Ian Katz, Jane Martinson, Sarah Phillips, Sarah Hewitt, Kira Cochrane, Stephen Moss, Jon Henley, Will Woodward and Aditya Chakrabortty.

The friendship of the following means a lot: Natasha Lennard, Jacob Goodwin, Olivia Sudjic, Lizzie Crarer, Bethan Bide, Imogen Walford, Ed Blain, Hugo Gye, Michael Derringer, Jim Kitchen, Ed Kiely, Dave Allen, Stuart McPherson, Nick and Sally Welsh, Jenni Russell and Jessica Lambert.

Ralegh Long, Jonathan Sebire, David Story, Alex Clatworthy, Jessica Riches all helped with transcription. Laura Pauling gave me some great economics know-how.

A special shout-out to Troels Leth Petersen's company, Running Tours Copenhagen. Highly recommended to all Copenhagen visitors who like to mix culture and fitness.

To everyone I've forgotten: sorry. And thank you.

INDEX

Patrick Kingsley is a feature writer for *The Guardian*. He lives in London and this is his first book.